Bhagawad Geeta
The Gospel of Timeless Wisdom
[10-Part Lecture Series]

Yours To You

Bhagawad Geeta

The Gospel of Timeless Wisdom

[10-Part Lecture Series]

Commentary by :

PRABHA DUNEJA

Presented by :

GEETA SOCIETY

2822, Camino Segura

Pleasanton, CA 94566, U.S.A.

ISBN : 81-7077-080-7
First Edition : Jan., 2005
Second Edition : Apr., 2006
© All rights reserved with Commentator

PRABHA DUNEJA
2822, Camino Segura
Pleasanton, CA 94566, U.S.A.
Tel. : 925-484-5411; Fax : 925-417-5946
e-mail : duneja@aol.com
website : www.holygeeta.com

Editor :
Dr. Baldeo Sahai
Writer, Journalist and Fellow of Indian National Science Academy

Publisher :
GOVINDRAM HASANAND
4408, Nai Sarak, Delhi-110 006 (INDIA)
Tel. : 91-11-23977216
e-mail : ajayarya@vsnl.com
Web : www.vedicbooks.com

Printed at :
RADHA PRESS
2465, Main Road, Kailash Nagar, Delhi-110 031 (INDIA)

Contents

Publisher's Note

The Publisher feels privileged in presenting the lectures on Srimad Bhagawad Geeta—the Gospel of Timeless Wisdom—by Mrs. Prabha Duneja, an educationist and devotee of Lord Kṛṣṇa.

Prabha has authored a number of books. Her clarity of vision about the teachings of the Geeta and her humility makes her a great teacher. She comes from a family of Vedic scholars, specially her father and uncle, who dedicated their whole lives to the study and preaching of the Vedas and Vedanta. She is blessed with divine gifts and talents and is a featured speaker at temples, churches, schools and at conferences—introducing the Vedic philosophy and the message of the Geeta in the USA and other parts of the world.

Designed especially for modern generation, this book is ideal for anyone seeking to replace inner stress with inner peace, and needs guidance, grace and inspiration in daily life.

I am sure that the compiled version of the series of lectures on the gospel of inspired action will receive a warm reception from the general public, as have the author's earlier works.

—Publisher

Acknowledgements

My sincere gratitude goes to the revered Guru the ancient sage Ved Vyasa who compiled the holy words of Lord Kṛṣṇa and passed on to us the timeless teachings of Bhagawad Geeta.

I am particularly grateful to my husband Amritji and our son Anshuman for their genuine encouragement and sincere support in the completion of this noble work. I want to express my heartfelt gratitude to my respected grandparents Sri and Smt. Ganga Ramji, my parents Dr. and Mrs. Manohar Lalji and my uncle Prof. Nand Lalji who initiated me in the study of Vedic literature and Bhagawad Geeta at the early age of eight. I am extremely grateful to Dr. Baldeo Sahai, a renowned scholar, to go through the pages of this book. A Fellow of the Indian National Science Academy, member of Indian Information Service, a journalist, poet, art critic and author of several books, he has also been generous to give a Foreword to the volume. Special thanks to my dear friend Manorama Iyer, who generously offered her time and skill in typing to prepare the final text.

—**Prabha Duneja**

Foreword

Prabha Duneja is the uncrowned ambassador of Lord Kṛṣṇa's Geeta. Brought up in Vedic lore since childhood, she chose Geeta as her guide early in life. She has established a Geeta Society in California where she is settled, prepared a set of audio-cassettes on the Geeta and has been tirelessly giving lectures on the sublime philosophy of the Holy book. Herself soaked in the teachings of Lord Kṛṣṇa, her writings have a ring of sincerity.

The essence of Geeta is that man is Divine. To attain the state of Divinity, Lord Kṛṣṇa suggests several ways to suit different temperaments. Emotional people may opt for the path of love or devotion. Men of action may engage themselves in the unselfish service of God's creatures. The intellectuals may go in for *Jñāna Mārg*. The author feels that all paths finally lead to ardent love for God and complete surrender to Him.

At one point in Chapter III, Lord Kṛṣṇa explains the hierarchy of human faculties. He says that senses are more powerful than the body; higher than senses is the mind; superior to mind is the intellect and higher than intellect is the *Atma*. Lord Yama, the God of Death, in Kathopanisad, extending the chain says that beyond the Atma is *Mahat, Hiranyagarbha*. Higher than that is *avyakta*, the unmanifest, the seed of all creation; and beyond this final cause, is the causeless Cause, the unmoved Mover, the Purusha—The same has been confirmed later in chapter XV by Lord Kṛṣṇa.

The bane of mankind is that it is stuck at 'intellect', and thinks that there is no faculty higher than that. Little do we realize that intellect is not a very reliable faculty. What is transient, the intellect sees as permanent; what will lead to unhappiness we regard as the fountain of happiness; what is unreal, we think as real, *satya*. We have to rise above 'intellect' to the level of Cosmic Intelligence and, through meditation, acquaint ourselves with still higher faculties, finally getting absorbed in Purusha.

Prabha advocates that one can awaken all the latent human faculties through deep devotion to God. She has explained this philosophy in several publications and repeated her emphasis on devotion and practical experience. In 1998, she published her magnum opus—*The Legacy of Yoga in Bhagawad Geeta.* In over 600 pages, it carries complete text of Geeta in Roman transliteration, with its faithful translation, and elaborate commentary in lucid English.

A selection of her lectures is now being brought out as Bhagawad Geeta : *The Gospel of Timeless Wisdom.* When there are already many commentaries on the Geeta— and she herself has written one critique—one may ask why yet another book on the same subject. In *The Legacy of Yoga,* the author was circumscript by the text of the *shlokas* and had little space to step out. This book enjoys a sense of abandon. There is a free flow of ideas. The author does cover the basic philosophy contained in the eighteen chapters of the Geeta but the expression is not cramped by the text of the verse.

Moreover, this book contains a lot of additional material. For example, the observations of Maharishi Mahesh Yogi, that the nine parts of DNA have their counterparts in the nine planets, is very interesting. He also adds that the twenty-seven groups of nucleic acid found in the cell, correspond to constellations. The author has explained here exhaustively the psychic centres rising from Kundalini—The Serpent Power—at the base of spine to the crown of the head. The awakening of Kundalini, however, should be taken up only under the guidance of a Guru.

Whereas *The Legacy of Yoga in Bhagawad Geeta* is to be treated as a book of reference, the present handy volume may well be prescribed in schools and colleges for the students of philosophy. The general public will also find this concise book very informative and immensely readable.

September. 2004   **—Dr. Baldeo Sahai**

Fellow, Indian National Science Academy,
Founder President, Upanisad Society,
New Delhi.

Introduction

The perennial philosophy of Bhagawad Geeta has been a rich source of guidance, enlightenment and inspiration to the entire mankind for centuries. It is one of the few scriptures of the world which clearly explains the cherished principles and practices of the gospel of inspired action. It is a compendium of timeless wisdom which combines the understanding of mind, body and spirit; sets forth in straightforward language the essential steps towards self-transformation. The philosophical concepts contained in the Vedas, Upanishads and in later works like Patanjali Yogasutra are beautifully blended in Srimad Bhagawad Geeta. The holy dialogue presents a complete vision of both the theoretical knowledge of the Supreme Divinity (Brahma Vidya) and also that of the Yoga Sastra—the techniques to perceive and experience the transcendental reality which is the substratum of the universe. The philosophical message of Geeta guides the individual to enter the higher path of living where he can improve the quality of life and be introduced to his inherent potential.

Sri Kṛṣṇa enlightens Arjuna with the mysteries of yogic unity and how a person becomes wise just by learning to live in the awareness of the Higher-Self. He repeats several times during the dialogue *"tasmat sarvesu kalesu yogayukto bhava Arjuna",*—O'Arjuna, remain aware of the yogic unity with the Self and do all your work with the guidance of the Self. Right alignment of mind, body and spirit under all circumstances is indeed a necessity of life. Yoga is perpetual anchorage with the source of life and Karmayoga is the manifestation of anchorage in the activities of day-to-day life. Karmayoga is definitely an extraordinary spiritual practice. He tells Arjuna that everything in our day-to-day life evolves around the games of mind and unless the mind is anchored to the indwelling Supreme-Self, an individual will continue to err. It is necessary, therefore, to learn to live in the consciousness of the soul, perceive pure intelligence within the range of conscious mind and infuse purity of Divine nature into the activities of daily life. Accelerate awareness, rise above the field of conditioned thinking and experience the influence of the Superconscious even in the ordinary functions of day-to-day life. With alignment to the source of life, clarity of vision improves rapidly and retrieval of memory becomes more pronounced. Ordinary work is performed with extraordinary efficiency and enthusiasm. Exceptional functional skills and extraordinary abilities become more evident. Peaceful, spiritualized and integrated living becomes a way of life and mind remains alert and attentive to the call of Divine.

This series of lectures is compiled from many discourses on Bhagawad Geeta, I have shared with the admirers of Geeta and Vedic philosophy at temples, universities, churches, conferences and religious gatherings. Designed especially for the modern generation, this elegant volume features a simple format, crisp summary of each chapter with new titles in modern English for people in today's world. The ancient wisdom of the East has been synthesized with modern approach of the West. This book is ideal for anyone trying to understand the inner meaning of the Holy dialogue and receive guidance, grace and inspiration in daily life. While sharing my understanding of Geeta I have often felt the living presence of Lord Krsna behind His holy words—as God incarnate, the protector of Dharma (righteousness) a compassionate and caring friend of Arjuna and His devotees, the greatest teacher of the universe and the Supreme Purusha.

May the teachings of Bhagawad Geeta bless every one with the power of enlightened love, devotion and true knowledge. May the words of Lord Krsna touch the heart of entire mankind—restoring peace, happiness and harmony on earth.

January 14th, 2005   —*Prabha Duneja*
Pleasanton, CA, U.S.A.

The Glory of
Srimad Bhagawad Geeta

"Among the priceless teachings that may be found in the great Hindu poem of the *Mahabharata,* there is none, so rare and precious as this 'The Lord's Song'. Since it fell from the divine lips of Sri Kṛṣṇa on the field of battle, and stilled the surging emotions of the disciple and friend, how many troubled hearts has it quietened and strengthened, how many weary souls has it led to Him ! It is meant to lift the aspirant from the lower levels of renunciation, where objects are renounced, to the loftier heights where desires are dead, and where the Yogi dwells in calm and ceaseless contemplation while his body and mind are actively employed in discharging the duties that fall to his lot in life. That the spiritual man need not be a recluse, that union with divine life may be achieved and maintained in the midst of worldly affairs, that the obstacles to that union lie, not outside us, within us, such is the central lesson of the Bhagawad Geeta."   —*Dr. Annie Besant*

"This ancient book can satisfy the modern needs. Nearly every literate yogi in India carries with him a small edition of this inspired and profound classic, the Bhagawad Geeta. If this gospel of contemplation combined with action had been understood in the land of its birth as it should be understood, India would today shed the radiance of her spiritual illumination to the far corners of the world and provide a masterly pattern of a balanced material-spiritual existence for all other countries to witness. The Geeta summarizes various approaches to the Over-self and also describes the latter. Sri Kṛṣṇa not only represents the embodied spiritual teacher, He is ultimately the Over-self within man, the God within who can illuminate all dark corners and answer all questions. At the end of the dialogue after hearing all the teachings, the pupil's mind becomes peaceful. He says indeed : 'My doubts are dispelled. Destroyed are my illusions'. By what magic was this mental change accomplished? Through both the guidance and grace received from his teacher and his own inner growth in striving for insight. The difficulties one meets in modern life can be met and overcome after we gain such insight. Wisdom means the ability to negotiate all the circumstances of life adequately, correctly and with spiritual success. The deep spiritual comfort emanating from the teachings of the Geeta is peculiarly needed at this stage of the world's affairs."

—*Dr. Paul Brunton*

"I believe that in all the living languages of the world, there is no book so full of true knowledge, and yet so handy as the Bhagawad Geeta".

—*Sri Madan Mohan Malaviya*

"The Geeta is one of the clearest and most comprehensive summaries of the Perennial Philosophy ever to have been done. Hence its enduring value, not only for Indians, but for all mankind.... The Bhagawad Geeta is perhaps the most systematic spiritual statement of the Perennial Philosophy".   —*Aldous Huxley*

"In the morning I bathe my intellect in the stupendous and cosmogonal philosophy of the Bhagawad Geeta, since whose composition years of the gods have elapsed, and in comparison with which our modern world and its literature seem puny and trivial."   —*Henry David Thoreau*

"I owed a magnificent day to the Bhagawad Geeta. It was the first of books; it was as if an empire spoke to us, nothing small or unworthy but large, serene, consistent, the voice of an old intelligence which in another age and climate had pondered and thus disposed of the same questions which exercise us".   —*Ralph Waldo Emerson*

It is knowledge of this mystic truth which makes man omnipotent, makes him master of the universe, and so "Free"; free, that is, from the limitations and annoyances of finite life.   —*Franklin Edgerton*

"When doubts haunt me, when disappointments stare me in the face, and I don't see any ray of hope on the horizon, I turn to Bhagawad Geeta and find a verse to comfort me; and I immediately begin to smile in the midst of overwhelming sorrow".   —*Mahatma Gandhi*

"Geeta is a first-hand guide to the ancient roots of Vedic religion. Although in *Shevatshvatara Upanisad* the transcendence of the personal God has been affirmed to some extent, with Geeta has come the devotional religion".

—*Dr. R.C. Zaehner*

"When the British Empire is lost in oblivion, when its sources of wealth and prosperity are not remembered, this scripture and lessons it contains will continue to inspire millions of people in this world. "   —*Warren Hastings*

First British Governer General of India

"The dramatic moral crisis that is central to the Bhagawad Geeta has inspired centuries of Indian philosophers and practical men of wisdom, as well as Western thinkers such as Thoreau, Emerson and Eliot. Interpretations of the Geeta, as it is commonly referred to in India, are as varied as the figures who have commented on it. From Sankara, the great Hindu philosopher of the eighth century, to Mahatma Gandhi, the leader of India's independence struggle in the twentieth century, each thinker has emphasized the path to spiritual liberation that was suited to his view of reality. These various interpretations reflect the intentionally multifaceted message of Sri Krsna's teaching.

Among the many works of Asian literature that were studied in Concord, Massachusetts, in the mid-nineteenth century, none was more influential than the Bhagawad Geeta".   —*Barbara Stoler Miller*

"For centuries people have found comfort in this great book which sets forth in precise and penetrating words the essential principles of a spiritual religion which are not contingent on ill-founded facts, unscientific dogmas or arbitrary fancies. With long history of spiritual power, it serves even today as a light to all who will receive illumination from the profundity of its wisdom which insists on a world wider and deeper than wars and revolutions can touch. It is a powerful shaping factor in the renewal of spiritual life and has secured an assured place among the world's greatest scriptures."   —*Dr. S. Radhakrishnan*

"The incomparable religious classic of India. So lofty are many of its declarations, so sublime its aspirations, so pure and tender its piety, ...that English literature would certainly be incomplete without possessing in popular form, a poetical and philosophical work so dear to India. "
                                        —*Sir Edwin Arnold*

The Geeta is a bouquet composed of the beautiful flowers of spiritual truths collected from the Upanishads.
                                        —*Swami Vivekananda*

1

Self and Supreme-Self
&
Reincarnation

Bhagawad Geeta, Chapter 1 & 2
Vishadyoga & Samkhyayoga

Self and Supreme-Self :

Bhagawad Geeta, the Gospel of timeless wisdom, is the holy dialogue between Arjuna and Lord Kṛṣṇa. Geeta presents the journey of the human-soul from a confused and depressed state of mind to the realization of the Self. The dialogue opens with Arjuna's depression and is concluded with surrender in God, when his depressed mind becomes receptive to the voice of God and he wakes up to the essential nature of the Supreme-Self. Arjuna who was engrossed in depression and loneliness wakes up into a blissful state of inner peace, integration and happiness. Life that

seemed a burden to him becomes a blessing. This is the experience of Holy Communion and discovery of life. It is being awakened to one's own divinity and the field of infinite possibilities. Geeta presents a symbolic picture of constant battle between the forces of darkness and light; between the conditioned egocentric-self and pure-self. This philosophical message is not only addressed to Arjuna for his immediate problems, but to the entire mankind about the nature of performing action, the meaningful purpose of life and the insight demanded of us to solve the basic problems of life. Throughout the dialogue, Sri Krṣṇa enlightens Arjuna with the mysteries of yogic unity and the importance of learning to live in the awareness of Supreme-Self and work in copartnership with God. Here Arjuna is guided step by step through the conditioned intrigues of mind into the clear understanding of the Absolute Truth. Arjuna comes to realize that he is actually a co-sharer in accomplishing the restoration of Dharma and orderliness in times of great chaos in society.

The dialogue includes in depth the psychological effects of teachings on human consciousness and the subjective changes that occur with devoted and receptive attitude of Arjuna. Throughout the long conversation between Sri Krṣṇa and Arjuna, there are other substantive ideas related not so much to the immediate problem of

The individual-soul enclosed within the mind with *pranna* and *tejas* keeps entering into new life guided by the thoughts, desires and samskaras.

— Prasna Upnishad 3.1

Arjuna but which have a profound bearing on the process of Self-revelation and Self-realization.

The message of the holy dialogue is phenomenal. It presents a profound insight into the workings of human nature and also provides guidance which is needed in every field of life. A simple and straightforward approach towards the understanding of the Self at various levels of human consciousness makes the dialogue really unique. It is a journey from the subtle to the gross from the subconscious to the conscious and from the unmanifest to the manifested Divinity. Sri Kṛṣṇa enlightens Arjuna about the knowledge of the Supreme-Self along with the proper understanding of the individual-self. It is through the art of developing a communion with the Higher-Self, the embodied-self becomes enlightened about the various levels of consciousness such as physical-self, psychological-self and the spiritual-self. It is intimacy with the Supreme-soul which marks the fundamental basis for the acquaintance with everything that exists within and without. The knowledge of the Self which comes in the form of increased intuition guides the individual about the proper functioning in life is in fact experiential. It is not revealed to a person at random, it comes in a very systematic order. It emerges from the deepest awareness and moves through the various levels of consciousness. When the mind turns inward for guidance, the inner chamber of subconscious mind starts opening one by one and the change takes place in person's personality step by step.

The teachings of Geeta are universal—meant for the welfare of the whole universe. It is an age-long repository of almost all the well-known teachings of ancient scriptures of the world and it is addressed to the entire mankind. Bhagawad Geeta has been called a Yoga Sastra. The word yoga has been derived from the Sanskrit root word *Yuj* which literally means to bind, combine and join together various levels of consciousness to experience a union and communion with the Supreme-Self. It is an art which helps a person to bring his scattered thoughts together into a reflective and meditative state of mind to comprehend the presence of the Divinity within. Yoga is the unity of the individual-soul *(Jivatma)* with the Supreme-Soul *(Paramatma)*. It is the communication of the individual-self with the Higher-Self. Yogic discipline is a systematic practice of exploring the inner dimensions of our personality and ultimately being introduced to our own-selves and others. The art of living in yoga improves the quality of life; gives self-respect, self-confidence and positive control over the activities of our mind and body. It disciplines our lives and prepares us step by step for the habit of living in the consciousness of the Divine. It re-orients the entire personality where the thoughts, words and actions blend into a homogeneous whole. It helps us to develop a special ability of maintaining the presence of mind under all circumstances in life. It promotes creativity, clarity and precision of thoughts.

According to ancient scriptures, yoga system was introduced by the sage Patanjali. It describes one hundred and ninety five sutras divided into four sections. The first part deals with the theory of yoga; the second with the art of Yoga and initiation into practice. The third describes the method of comprehending the inherent powers and the fourth deals with inner unity in meditation. The Patanjali Yoga Sutra also describes the eight steps of self-discipline for going into union and communion with God. Bhagawad Geeta, the holy dialogue, has been called a Yogasastra because it explains the theoretical knowledge of the Soul and also the techniques to experience the unity with the Soul. The colophon *Srimadbhagawadgeetasupanisatsu brahmavidyayam yogasastre*—towards the end of each chapter clearly indicates that Bhagawad Geeta is the science of Absolute—Supreme Parabrahmn and the great scripture of yoga. It is both the knowledge of the Supreme reality and the art of union with that reality which permeates the entire universe of plurality. The entire yogic philosophy written by any sage has been summarized in the holy sermon. The concept of yoga as described in Geeta is very subtle, broad, flexible and comprehensive, all at the same time. Here the aspirant is initiated to live his entire life in the awareness of the self and perform all his work under the perpetual guidance of unity in yoga. It is to live a life which is firmly grounded in eternal union with the Supreme-Soul and working with the consciousness of the indwelling self.

Sri Kṛṣṇa has used many expressions in order to explain the subtle meaning of yoga to Arjuna—such as Nityayoga, Jñānayoga, Samatvamyoga, Karmayoga, Bhaktiyoga, Rajyoga, Abhyasyoga, Jaapyoga, Karma-Sannyasayoga and Dhyanayoga.

The subtle meaning of all these terms is to initiate a person into a life of yogic unity with the Higher-Self, which guides him into a higher systematic peaceful, creative, productive, enjoyable and balanced life style. The message of Geeta makes it very clear that the unity in Yoga is not merely a practice in isolation; it is the discipline of living in the consciousness of the Self. Yoga is the manifestation of inner unity in every day life. It is the experience of living in bliss which comes to us with a disciplined daily practice and gradually grows from moment to moment. It is indeed true that there is no other book so inspiring, so enlightening, so refreshing, so absorbing in which, the understanding of the relationship between the mind, body and spirit is renewed every time we read. The perennial message of self-knowledge through alignment with the indwelling Supreme-Soul is expressed marvellously. It is interesting, appealing, comprehensive and replete with profound wisdom, truths and mysteries of life.

The concept of yoga is presented with exceptional clarity, simplicity and depth. The Geeta presents the most wonderful guidance for self-realization and God realization. Throughout the long dialogue there is not a single *Shloka* which lacks interest and not a single one which any one would like to skip. There is a special emphasis on the transcendental remoteness of the Divine as well as the loving intimacy of the Lord. The presence of Sri Kṛṣṇa is felt and perceived behind His words. In the entire dialogue one perceives the subtle gleam of Divinity and the spiritual mystery of Lord Kṛṣṇa—as God incarnate; the protector of Dharma (righteousness) the compassionate and caring friend of Arjuna; the speaker of the holy sermon and the greatest teacher of the world. This mesmeric touch of the Lord makes the dialogue simply unique.

The most luminous dialogue in Geeta opens with *Vishadyoga*. *Vishad* means sadness and deep sorrow. It is a depressed state of mind when everything in life appears to be unsettled and confused. In moments of loneliness, when we feel helpless and depressed, we are persuaded to seek help from God and take refuge in Him. Communion with the indwelling Lord in moments of depression is called *Vishadyoga*. An honest surrender to the Supreme Lord in pain and innocence is indeed *Vishadyoga*. It is for sure a fact that when a person cries out for help from the purity of his heart, the guidance comes from the God in us. Any painful serious and traumatic experience of life brings the internal guidance which helps the person to release the painful past and move on in life with a new concept of truth. It is like making progress from one stage to another; moving from darkness to light; from less awareness to increased awareness and from bondage to freedom. Every person has to pass through the self created egocentric boundaries of 'I and Mine' in order to comprehend the blissful experience of communion with the Higher-Self. It is in *Vishad*—sadness and pain—when we have the blessed experience of the Holy Communion with the indwelling Lord; it is in *Vishad,* when we are guided from the source of life in us. As a matter of fact *Vishad* is a blessing in disguise and the Lord's unique way of helping us for inner enlightenment.

Reincarnation :

Arjuna detracts from his assigned duty and feels helpless. Self-pity is an expression of emotional weakness, which generally perpetuates the situation. It is the cry of a heart which is ruled by conflicting emotions. The expression *Karpanyadosopahata-svabhavah*—indicates the truth that Arjuna is aware of his confusion. He says, O'Kṛṣṇa! Please tell me, which is decidedly good for me— I am your disciple, I have taken refuge in You and I need your help. Please teach me and guide me as to whatever is by all means good for me.

Arjuna knows that his inner conflict is serious and he definitely needs some help. As a matter of fact, to accept confusion and ask for help is indeed the most important step towards self-realization. Sri Kṛṣṇa the knower of human psychology, remains quiet so far and he simply listens to all what Arjuna has to say. It is only after Arjuna makes a request for help that he opens the conversation. 'O Arjuna—the soul is immortal'. He explains that the entire manifestation of Supreme Para-brahman represents the real and unreal, absolute and relative, the non-changing and the changing, the immortal and the mortal, the Supreme-Self and the conditioned-self. The real is eternal, and the unreal is ever changing and perishable.

To understand the essential nature of the Self, we

have to learn about the difference between real and unreal, the pure consciousness and the conditioned consciousness. The real always remains the same while the unreal changes every moment. Everything that comes into existence, is sustained for a while and then it is gone—but there is one unchanging reality that prevails at the heart of entire universe. It is the Supreme consciousness, the Supreme-soul and the essential being of everything living and non-living. The *asat* or unreal is within the comprehension of human mind, that's why the mind interprets everything in the world in relation to unreal. Everybody lives his life, with the notion of accepting unreal to be real, and the transitory to be permanent. The ordinary human mind with its finite powers can't grasp the difference between the *sat* and *asat*. But the wise sage who lives in consciousness of the Divine has the experiential knowledge of both existent and nonexistent. He transcends the limitations of the mind and body and lives in the blissful state of *Sat-chit-anand.* The man of wisdom doesn't assign any reality to the transitory, ever changing things of the mundane world because he has realized the essence of both.

Sri Krṣna tells Arjuna that the body goes through all kinds of changes in life but the soul ever remains the same. Even at the time of death, soul goes from one body to another forced by thoughts and memories. The death is not an end in itself, it only marks the time for change and a new beginning. I like these words of Rabindranath Tagore from *Gitanjali,* "I was not aware of the moment when I first crossed the threshold of this life. What was the power that made me open out into this vast mystery like a bud in the forest at midnight! When in the morning I looked upon the light I felt in a moment that I was no stranger in this world. Even so, in death the same unknown will appear as ever known to me. And because I love this life, I know I shall love death as well". The soul of everyone existed in the past, exists in present and will exist in future. It merely changes name and form. Sri Kṛṣṇa makes reference to pre-existence and post-existence of the beings. He tells Arjuna that 'He Himself', and all the other kings have always existed in the past and will also continue to exist hereafter.

Sri Kṛṣṇa tells Arjuna that the different stages of body such as childhood, youth and old age simply indicate the changes in the physical body. The body goes through all kinds of growth and changes but the one who observes the entire change, the soul, always remains the same. The bodies have a beginning and an end. The Supreme-soul resides in the body as the embodied-soul. In due course of time when the body disintegrates, the soul gets out of that body and enters into another. The embodied-soul goes from one body to another, guided by the thoughts and memories which have been accumulated during the life time. The individual soul retains its individuality from one stage to another and also from one life to another. All sorts of changes take place only at the physical level and the unchangeable soul remains untouched. Destruction of the gross body can never cause any destruction in the continuity of the indestructible soul.

The soul at one time becomes someone's father, at another time, the son, the elder brother and yet another time the younger brother. One soul enclosed within the mind has gone through many births before, and keeps entering into new wombs. The process of understanding the nature of soul is really very subtle and difficult; it can not be described in words. Sri Kṛṣṇa gives some examples which are within the comprehension of human mind—the fire can not burn nor can water make it wet and also weapons can not cut it. It is eternal, all pervading, unchanging, immovable and primordial.

This reminds me of an interesting incident from the life story of Socrates. Before his death when he was asked as to how his death rituals should be performed, he replied amusingly—in any way you like, but first you must catch me, the real me. He always taught his followers about the immortality of soul. The saints and philosophers who live in the awareness of Soul, for them death is only a change, in which the soul leaves one body and enters into another which is new. They know clearly that the physical body was meant to live only for a limited time—between the two events—birth and death. The journey of soul is ever-renewing on the path of eternity. The doctrine of reincarnation, says Swami Chinmayananda, has been accepted by great sages, philosophers and prophets all round the world.

The Buddha constantly made references to his previous births. Virgil and Ovid regarded the doctrine as perfectly self-evident. Josephus observed that the belief in reincarnation was widely accepted among the Jews of his age. Solomon's *Book of Wisdom* says : "To be born in sound body with sound limbs is a reward of the virtues of the past lives". Origen, the most learned of the Christian Fathers, has clearly declared: "Every man received a body for himself according to his deserts in former lives". He further says, "The prodigy Mozart who wrote sonatas at the age of four, played in public at the age of five, definitely explains the continuity of the embodied-soul". The perennial cycle of birth, death and rebirth has been going on since the beginning of creation. Civilizations come and go, kingdoms rise and fall, stars and planets keep on breaking to move towards the inevitable change. This process is active in macrocosm as well as in microcosm. For example, every cell in the human body obeys the same law of creation, evolution and destruction as an atom does in the material universe. Millions and trillions of reactions take place in human body every single minute of life. Sri Vinobaji used to say that modern scientists believe that in seven years the whole body changes and not even a drop of the old blood remains.

The Vedic sages believed that the entire physical body changes in twelve years and is replaced by a new one. They declared the process as *Kaya Kalpa.* That is the reason why they fixed the period for *prayaschitta, tapasya* and *swadhayaya*—that is self purification, austerity and self-study as twelve years. Creation and destruction is an ongoing process in the stream of life which renews itself every single minute. Death is certain of the one who is born and rebirth is equally certain for the one who dies. The physical body is composed of material components that go through changes between two points of birth and death but the soul remains unchanged. It is due to the conditioned nature of the self that we forget our essentiality being immortal. We live this life surrounded by all types of fears because of our own ignorance and conditioned habits. It is really so true that most of our worries and fears in life can be eliminated if we could ever perceive our immortality. Our identification with mind and body takes away from us, the rich experience of being fearless, ageless, timeless and immortal. The moment we understand the difference between the body and soul, we are introduced to our unconditioned nature which brings freedom from all kinds of fears.

As a matter of fact, absolute truth about the soul is veiled in many layers of consciousness and is indeed difficult to comprehend. It is only at a specific level of awareness when a person goes beyond the boundaries of mind and body that he perceives the subtlety of the soul. He understands that although his body is confined in space and time but his true identity as the Supreme soul is not bound at all. He remains grounded in his deepest awareness and looks upon the creation as a play of matter and energy that flickers here and there creating new shapes and forms. He beholds changes governed by the law of nature in the physical body and accelerates himself to the level of realization which is not touched by any type of change.

It is indeed very difficult to educate some one about the essential nature of Soul. It has to be a personal experience. Although each and every person is an eligible candidate for the experiential knowledge of the Divine, still only few are blessed with it. The reason is that only few in many billions, are actually willing to pursue the path of God-realization. However still less are those who have the genuine urge, courage, determination and an insatiable desire to comprehend the essentiality of the Supreme-soul.

Sri Kṛṣṇa tells Arjuna that anyone who is settled in the pure unconditioned nature of soul, he naturally becomes settled in Dharma, truth, justice and universal unity. Subjective awareness of the Supreme-soul helps him to understand his expanded field of relationship which lies beyond the boundaries of mind and body. He becomes enlightened about his proper role as a member of the family and also a responsible member of the community and country at large. Anybody who remains centred in the unity with the Supreme-self follows the guidance of the Supreme, and the laws of *swadharma*. Living in harmony with the transcendental consciousness is indeed the real realization of human efforts.

Sri Kṛṣṇa reminds Arjuna to recollect his true identity and re-educate himself about the true nature of the soul and his own essential Divine nature. He wants Arjuna to re-evaluate the entire scenario on the basis of his connections with the indwelling soul and not from the viewpoint of his limited identification with the mind and body. He wants Arjuna to wake up to the reality of his essential being and realize the nature of the indwelling-self, which is immortal and immutable. Sri Kṛṣṇa persuades him to examine his attitude once again with renewed understanding. He wants him to be introduced to the unconditioned ever-luminous purity of the Supreme-Self and be fearless, unattached and integrated. He enthuses Arjuna to understand and realize the secret of performing his duty with inner peace, tranquillity, integrity and joy which is indeed the art of living in yoga. Sri Kṛṣṇa wants Arjuna to become aware of himself as an active, responsible citizen of the country and perform his duties with the guidance of the Supreme-Self. He reminds Arjuna about his unconditioned nature that is essentially pure and luminous. It brings harmony to the entire field of activity and glorifies life in all respects.

After declaring soul as immortal, immutable, omnipresent and ever existent, Sri Kṛṣṇa draws Arjuna's attention towards *swadharma* and the purpose of life. The word *swadharma* combines two words. The Sanskrit word *Swa*-means 'the indwelling light' and the word *Dharma*-means 'to hold or to maintain'. It is a unique system of values, determined and dictated by the inner self, which guides the person to perform his duties by keeping in mind global welfare. The concept of *swadharma* in Geeta indicates that this world is a *Dharmakshetra.* Every person should develop a sense of responsibility towards his own duty. He tells Arjuna that he should fight the battle in the spirit of service to his countrymen. If he fights with peace of mind, he will definitely make the right decision at the right moment. He tells Arjuna that he is not only a member of his family he is also a very important member of the community. He must learn to rise above conflicting emotions. Sri Kṛṣṇa makes it clear that although these feelings are natural, especially when we screen the reality through the ideas which are conditioned with some fixed notions. It is the attachment to that notion or fixed idea which becomes the cause of pleasure and pain.

Sri Kṛṣṇa enlightens Arjuna about the subtle meaning of Karmayoga. The word yoga has been derived from the Sanskrit word *'yuj'*-which literally means to bind, and join together various levels of consciousness, in order to experience a union and communion with God. Yoga is the conscious communion of the individual-soul with the Supreme-soul. Karmayoga means the work which is performed in conscious unity with the Divine in copartnership with God. Although the gospel of selfless action has been mentioned in the Vedas but the process has not been explained clearly, especially for an ordinary person who is a member of the family, society and still wants to be a Karmayogi. Sri Kṛṣṇa explains the process very clearly. He tells Arjuna that the discipline of yoga is a practice of living in the awareness of the Self. This inner discipline and inner unity makes the individual receptive to the voice of the Supreme Lord and initiates him into the performance of action in copartnership with God, and eventually his action becomes the yoga of action.

The person becomes very determined and resolute. Since he works with integral wisdom and stability, the results of his work are par excellence. A yogi works wonders because of his inner peace and inner integrity. His work is always performed meticulously. The unity in Yoga opens the door of inner intelligence to intuitive knowledge and to the transcendental experience of the Supreme-soul. He makes it very clear to Arjuna that the performance of duty with the consciousness of Divine definitely brings peace, satisfaction, enjoyment and freedom.

He alerts Arjuna to become aware of the activities of mind and screen the reality through his unity in yoga. He wants him to be fully conscious of the yogic unity with the Supreme-self before engaging in action. Sri Kṛṣṇa assures Arjuna that even the highest achievement of meditative unity is possible through the yoga of action; because the person works in constant unity with the Divine. Karmayoga is the art of living and working through the uninterrupted consciousness of the Supreme-soul. As a matter of fact, the work itself becomes its reward when it is performed intelligently and devotedly. For example, an artist can produce masterpiece of art, only if he gets totally absorbed in his work; without being worried about the possible fears of failure and rejection. It is indeed so true that when he is devotedly and sincerely absorbed in the entire process of performing his work, the results are bound to be astonishing, there is no doubt about it. The gospel of selfless action inspires the individual into the performance of work with proper attention, accuracy, and punctuality. The practice of working through unity in yoga helps the person to accomplish a great amount of work in the shortest span of time. Sri Kṛṣṇa tells Arjuna: *Yogah karmasu kausalam—* yoga is skill in action. The performance of work through unity in yoga is indeed the key to perfection in work. Any one who performs work with unity in Yoga, he is eventually released from all kinds of stress and worries and lives in peace, harmony and freedom. It is a fact that the highest goal of life can be actualized when the person is consciously established in yogic unity and when he himself becomes aware of the truth that he is living in it.

Living a life in the awareness of the Divine, and performing all work in the consciousness of the Divine is Karmayoga. It is the realization of God through the performance of actions. Sri Kṛṣṇa knows that Arjuna needs to be educated in the concept of Karmayoga, which is in fact initiated from the unity with the source of life.

In general the realization of the self comes from tuition and intuition. Tuition is learning and guidance from teachers and books etc. and intuition is the guidance from source of life. It is the faculty of direct perception which enables the person to be in touch with the deepest mysteries of the Self and experience the sudden insights of perennial wisdom that encompasses everything in the universe. All the subjective experiences are apprehended intuitively. Intuition is inner awakening, it is inner guidance and inner wisdom. When the mind is purified in yoga the atma-jñana—the knowledge of the Self is revealed spontaneously. He tells Arjuna that when the intellect becomes firmly grounded in Divine, the person becomes very intuitive, integrated and the concept of Karmayoga becomes quite clear to him. He gets guidance from the Supreme-Self, which helps him to go beyond the mire of delusion. The person becomes steady and feels integrated and determined within. He feels confident and self-reliant. He perceives the presence of a higher power and becomes receptive to its guidance and instructions. He enjoys being united in yoga and work through yoga. Sri Kṛṣṇa is emphasizing that in order to be in touch with inner guidance and grace, the person has to turn inward to his own resources and become receptive to the voice of the Supreme-Self.

After listening to the glories of inner wisdom and Karmayoga, Arjuna makes a request to know more about the man of wisdom who has been blessed with intuition and becomes firmly grounded in the pure unconditioned nature of the Supreme-Self. *Sthitaprajñasya* means the one who is firmly established in the para-jñana—knowledge of the Supreme-Self. Sri Kṛṣṇa tells Arjuna that the person who has the experiential knowledge of the transcendental-Self, he definitely shows the grace of his inner unity even in his day-to-day life. There is a beauty in his countenance satisfaction in his manners and harmony in his words. A man of integral wisdom, who is ever united in yoga, makes quick, firm, impartial and very determined decisions. He is highly intuitive and his discerning ability is remarkable. His decisions come from the purity of his heart. His lifestyle becomes a beacon light for others in society. The eloquence of his speech and the careful analysis of his views manifest the serenity of his mind because he remains ever connected with the source of integral wisdom.

To live in the enlightened state of mind is like living in eternity. He knows how to maintain his balance while facing the dualities of life. He regards pleasure and pain, gain and loss, honour and dishonour as the passing phases of life. In reference to this, I am reminded of an incident from the life story of Sri Ramakrishna. Once Sri

Ramakrishna who was the chief priest at the Kali Temple, Calcutta made some mistakes during Durga Pooja. The managing committee of the temple decided to get rid of him. So one of the temple officials came to Ramakrishna and ordered him to leave at once. Without the least sign of resentment Ramakrishna picked up his towel and quietly walked out of the room, where he had lived for the past twenty-six years. He had almost reached the gate of the temple premises when the temple officials came running and they begged—please stay! We beg you to stay. At this Ramakrishna smiled, turned around, and went back to his room and continued his discourse before his devotees, as if nothing unusual had happened. This is how the man of inner integrity and wisdom acts in his day-to-day life. He lives his life in the perennial peace and silence of the Self. His life becomes pure, enlightened and he carries that peace and wisdom wherever he goes. The man of integral wisdom becomes a source of divine grace and shares that grace with every single person he comes across.

A man settled in transcendental wisdom becomes purified; his life is very disciplined, regulated and organized. He knows how to live in the awareness of the Self and work through the unity in yoga. He performs his essential duties very efficiently and relapses into the stream of meditative bliss whenever he wants to. Endowed with such stability and inner contentment, it is all upto him whether he decides to live with the family and takes an active interest in social service, or totally renounces the world. For example, the sage Yajñvalkya decided to retire to the forest while King Janaka decided to rule his great empire. The king ruled his kingdom as an embodiment of the Divine.

While giving a description about the man of purified intellect Sri Kṛṣṇa presents a new insight to the understanding of life which becomes primarily subjected to the fulfilment of worldly enjoyment. Here he presents a rational survey, which describes the essentials of human nature. The message is, that the downfall of a man is indeed rooted in his infatuation for worldly temptations. He tells Arjuna, that a man who constantly thinks about the enjoyment and luxuries of the material world, naturally develops attachment for them; from attachment comes desire. When the desire is not fulfilled it makes him angry. From anger comes delusion; from delusion, confusion of memory; from confusion of memory the loss of reason and from loss of reason he falls. In our century, E.F. Schumacher has repeated the same words—a man driven by greed and envy loses the power of understanding and perceiving things as they really are. In that case, even his great achievements become his failures. If the whole society becomes infected by these vices, they may achieve astonishing things but they become increasingly incapable of solving the most elementary problems of day-to-day life. He further adds—"What is wisdom? Where it can be found? It can be read in numerous publications but it can be found only inside our own self. To be able to find it, first of all the person has to liberate himself from such masters as greed and envy. The stillness following liberation—even if only momentary—produces the insights of wisdom which are obtainable in no other way". It is definitely in the silence of meditative unity we become enlightened, intuitive and can improve the quality of life. Transcendental unity in meditation is indeed a necessity of life—just in order to live in peace and harmony with our own inner self and with others.

Sri Kṛṣṇa glorifies once again the practice of self-discipline and transcendental yogic unity which forms the foundation of all types of progress in material as well as in spiritual life. A self-disciplined person can accomplish the maximum amount of work with the minimum use of physical energy. It is by the practice of constant self control, he cultures within himself a new and awakened lifestyle which operates under the direct guidance of the indwelling Lord. His entire span of work functions from the core of his essential being. He performs his duties regularly, efficiently, and relapses into the stream of transcendental bliss whenever he wants to.

Sri Kṛṣṇa has used the word *muni* for the description of the sage who is enlightened and remains settled in the awareness of the Supreme-soul. *Mana* (mind) is a state of consciousness. When *mana* becomes liberated from the false identifications, and returns to its source; the mind takes refuge in the awareness of the transcendental-Self and becomes silent. When the *mana* (mind) settles into *mouna* (silence) the person is called a *mouni* or *muni*. The words *Brahmisthitih* and nirvana has been used for the man of transcendental wisdom who has attained liberation. *Brahmisthitih* literally means settled in the state of deepest consciousness in which the mind becomes firmly grounded in *Brahmi chetna*. It is the consciousness of perceiving the presence of the Lord within one's own self. It is the state of awareness in which the human soul goes back to its essential nature. The word Nirvana means the human soul going into unity with the Supreme-soul. A fragment merging into the wholeness, a drop becoming a part of the ocean. Nirvana is freedom from all the masks of the conditioned-self. Nirvana is going back into the essential unconditioned, pure, luminous nature of the Supreme-soul. Nirvana means total bliss.

One with the Supreme Divinity, let every man resolve to live happily for a hundred years or more, with the gospel of selfless action and with an attitude of service.

— *Isa Upnishad 1.2*

2

The Gospel of Selfless Action, The Concept of Swadharma & Meaning of Sannyasa

Bhagawad Geeta, Chapter 3, 4 & 5
Karmayoga, Jnana-Karmayoga & Karmasannyasayoga

The Gospel of Selfless Action:

With reference to the philosophy of Karmayoga, the dialogue opens with a question from Arjuna. He asks: O'Kṛṣṇa if the knowledge of the Supreme-Self and unity in yoga is the only means to the realization of the Self, then how could the gospel of selfless action be helpful? He makes a request for proper explanation. Sri Kṛṣṇa declares that in this world there are two types of spiritual disciplines, the yoga of knowledge and the yoga of action. The yoga of knowledge means the type of knowledge that helps us to go in unity with the Higher-Self; while the yoga of action means the type of work which helps us to have union and communion with God. Both, the yoga of action and the yoga of knowledge, do complement each other. A man of integral wisdom who is perpetually established in the unconditioned pure knowledge of the Self, definitely performs all his work in a copartnership with God. In his practice of devotion-cum-action, a spontaneous flow of inner awareness is perceived that permeates into the work of his day-to-day life. It ultimately prepares him for direct experience of unity in yoga. He tells Arjuna that a person has to blend both, the yoga of knowledge and the yoga of action, in order to achieve the highest fulfilment in any activity. Both the methods of yoga are interdependent. A person needs the proper knowledge of both in order to attain perfection in either. Yoga of knowledge initiates the individual into perennial unity with the source of life and transforms every activity into yoga of action, while Karmayoga is to perform each and every activity with proper knowledge and with an attitude of devotion. Both Sankhyayoga, or the yoga of knowledge, and Karmayoga revolve round the performance of action selflessly and skilfully. In both the methods a great deal of sacrifice and self-discipline is mandatory. He explains to Arjuna that the method of self-realization and God-realization through the gospel of Karmayoga has been brought to the attention of mankind at the very beginning of creation. "Live a life with the spirit of yajña" is all about sacrifice—means to give and share. Yajña, a well known religious term of vedic tradition, literally means the work which helps the person to live in harmony with his own inner-self, with others and with nature.

The word yajña (sacrifice) indicates mutual dependence. It conveys the idea of interdependence, continuity and the survival of creation. It is the net work of the services, performed selflessly by human beings, gods, the other species, plants, trees, water bodies, stars and planets. Sri Kṛṣṇa explains the process of God-realization through the work performed as 'yajña' (sacrifice). In order to teach people the concept of yajña and how it can help them to live in harmony with others and with nature, the ancient vedic tradition has described five types of yajñas. Brahma-yajña, Deva-yajña, Pitri-yajña, Atithi-yajña and Bhuta-yajña. Accepting the omniscience of the Supreme Lord in the entire creation is Brahma-yajña. It is to live in the awareness of the Supreme Divinity and to share that experience with others. It is to become enlightened and in turn enlighten the lives of others.

The second type of yajña is Deva yajña which is to live in harmony with others and with the cosmic powers of nature. All the cosmic powers (devatas) are constantly giving to others in order to make life possible on the planet. It is the duty of every person to make the appropriate use of these blessings. Any type of negligence brings calamities such as famine, earthquake, drought, epidemics and storms etc. For example, the basic reason for almost all the present ecological problem is that people have forgotten their duties toward nature and toward others. In order to live in harmony with nature and to get full support of nature, we have to realize our duty at the personal as well as at the community level. All efforts for keeping the air clean and healthy and living in harmony with nature is Deva yajña. Sri Kṛṣṇa says, *"parasparam bhavayantah sreyah paramavapsyatha"*— means by fostering each other with mutual respect you will attain the highest good.

The third type of yajña is the 'Pitriyajña'. Pitra is a Sanskrit word which means the elders in family and ancestors. Living with the spirit of sacrifice in a family is pitri-yajña which prepares the person for living in peace and harmony with other people in society as well. The stability of a family unit contributes a lot to the peace and happiness of the community and country. Atithi yajña means giving due respect to the person who knocks at our door without any prior information. The fifth one is Bhuta yajña. The word *bhuta* stands for all living beings. Bhuta yajña describes the ideal of living in harmony with other creatures on earth. Vedic literature declares that each and every individual should develop a sense of responsibility towards the well being of other species on earth. Everything in the nature is meant to be shared with animals, birds and the plant kingdoms.

Sri Kṛṣṇa tells Arjuna that the entire universe is mutually connected. The entire work order in nature is closely related to the activities of human beings. The reservoirs of earth should be used wisely. The mother earth can definitely satisfy the basic needs of every one but not the greed of people. For example, if the man keeps chopping down the trees because he needs wood for fuel and housing, that day is not far off when the whole mankind will face a shortage of wood, food and rain. The green forests and trees increase the volume of water and the volume of water increases the volume of food. As Tolstoy, a great Russian scholar, has written "Work produces food, food produces work, the one is the consequence and cause of the other".

Modern science also believes in the same ideology. The fundamental concept of physics is that when an electron moves, the whole universe moves, because everything in the universe is interconnected. It is the combined movement of every little atom and every little molecule, that keeps the wheel of creation in motion, where everything and every body contribute in some way or the other. The spirit of yajña creates harmony in the entire universe. It is the realization of mutual interdependence and the attitude of service toward the entire creation. The performance of work in the spirit of yajña helps people understand the ideals of selfless action. It is the spirit of yajña which prepares the person for yogic communion with God. By drawing the similarities of macrocosm and microcosm, Sri Kṛṣṇa explains to Arjuna that all our activities must correspond to the world-order. Each and everybody should develop a sense of responsibility towards one's own duty. Human beings with their subjective awareness have the ability to stay aligned with the inner voice and receive the needed guidance from God. The indwelling voice guides everyone to perform his assigned duties by keeping in mind the global welfare. He declares that every individual, who is a member of family, society and country, should understand his duty at the personal level as well as at the universal. Anyone who fails to realize his duty lives a degraded, shameful and harmful life at the individual and also at the universal level. Sri Kṛṣṇa enlightens Arjuna about the personal responsibility of every person in order to live in harmony with nature and with other people.

He tells Arjuna that the Yoga of selfless action is not a new concept. This discipline of action came with the creation. The whole creation functions through the spirit of mutual interdependence. It is a network of services performed selflessly. Sri Kṛṣṇa tells Arjuna that an enlightened person can clearly see the ideology of yajña in all the functions of mother nature since the beginning of creation. The sun rises at its own predetermined hour and starts serving the creation. So is the case of the moon, the rain, the rivers and trees; in fact everything is working in harmony with one another, in order to serve life on the planet. The man of wisdom understands the meaning *"paropkarayarth phalanti vrikshsa, paropkarayarth dohanti gavah, paropkarayarth vahanti nadia, paropkarayarth midam shariram"*—the trees bear the fruits for the welfare of others, the cows give milk for the welfare of others, the rivers are flowing constantly for the welfare of others, my life is also meant for the service of others. He knows that it is expected from every person to earn money by appropriate means and make appropriate charities. For example, Dravyayajña is performed by donating a part of our income for the construction of hospitals, schools, orphanages, shrines, free lodging places along highways, libraries and water tanks etc. In this type of yajña the fund-raising dinners are organized to collect money for welfare of the community. The orphanages are supported to provide quality life and quality education to the orphans. The saints and other learned scholars are supported; those who are trying to enlighten the society with spiritual teachings. Such types of services help the individual to maintain a balance in society. It gives self-satisfaction, promotes the spirit of sharing and helps us in self-realization and God-realization.

Man is a social being and as a part of the family, society and nation, he has to play various roles. Performing the assigned work in the spirit of service brings purification and makes us receptive to the attainment of the higher goals. The self-realized person performs all his obligatory duties as husband, wife, mother, father, teacher and son just as a service to others. He does his work diligently and enthusiastically with the ideal of sharing and giving. His work is performed as yajña and as an offering to the Divine. Such an individual helps in the continuation of the world order and also gets enlightened while doing his duties. It is like working through God and working with God.

With reference to the principle of Karmayoga—the work which is performed with proper knowledge, insight and devotion, Swami Vivekanand has given a very good example. Once a young sannyasi went to a forest with the goal of self-realization. After long meditation and yoga practices, one day while he was sitting under a tree, some dry leaves fell upon his head. He felt very angry. He saw two birds on the tree fighting with each other. While he looked up, a flash of fire went out and killed the birds. He felt very proud about the advancement of his yogic powers. After few days he had to go to a nearby town to beg for some food. He stopped at a door and called out for food— "Some food please". As he called, a voice came from inside the house, please wait. The young sannyasi got upset and repeated once again in anger, 'food' please. A voice came again "Please don't think too much about your yogic powers; I'm neither your birds nor the leaves. The young sannyasi felt surprised at the sharp insight of the woman. Finally when the lady of the house came at the door he said—I salute and bow to you, please tell me how you knew all about my great adventure. She replied very politely, I'm a simple house-wife. My house is my temple and the work is my worship. I requested you to wait, because I've been taking care of my husband who is sick. I do all my work very devotedly, lovingly and as a service to the Divine. My devoted service has enlightened my life. I feel consciously settled in God and perform all my work as a service to God. This is karmayoga, the yoga of action, which sets the guidelines for self-realization and God-realization. This is an inspired level of consciousness which wraps in itself both the absolute and relative fields of life.

Sri Kṛṣṇa tells Arjuna that a person does not have to renounce the world in order to make spiritual advancement; because performance of duties with love, devotion and

detachment itself purifies the individual. It is the practice
of devotion-cum-action which educates the person in all
respects without fail. When a person learns to perform his
duties with proper knowledge and undivided devotion, the
procedure itself modifies the behaviour. Actually the
process itself becomes both the training and the teacher.

After listening in detail about the yoga of knowledge
and the yoga of action, Arjuna comes up with another
question, "O'Krsna, why a man becomes involved in
committing sin even though he doesn't want to? What
compels him to do which is prohibited by the code of
ethics and should not be done at all?" Sri Krsna gives a
precise answer. *Kama esa krodhah esarajagunsamudh-
bhavah*—means passionate desire and anger are insatiable
and most sinful. A passionate desire can definitely confuse
the understanding of a person. With reference to this, there
is a story told by Swami Chinmayananda, "Once a young
man was travelling in a train. On one platform a beautiful
young lady boarded his compartment. The man looked at
her, and gave her a friendly smile. She brought along a
huge box of quite unusual dimension. The lady looked at
the young man and said, "Sir, if you don't mind, may I
keep this box here". The man replied Oh' sure. The lady
sat next to the young man for a while and then went some
where else. He looked at the huge box and decided to bear

the inconvenience. He amused himself with the thoughts of the wonderful journey in the sweet company of the beautiful lady. But the lady did not return. The box was causing a lot of inconvenience for other passengers as well. After a little while a railway officer entered the compartment and queried about the box. All the other passengers pointed towards the young man. The officer suggested him to buy an extra luggage ticket. The young man, who was totally lost in the thoughts of the beautiful lady, quietly accepted the receipt and dropped it in his pocket. After a few hours the young man's station of destination arrived. He was still lost in the thoughts of the lady, and expected to see her at the railway station. So he decided to take the box with him. As he walked through the exit, a railway officer asked him to declare the contents of that box. The young man presented the luggage receipt. The officer asked for the key to open the box. When he refused to open, the officer became suspicious and told him to come to the police station. At the police station they opened the box, and found a dead body inside. The young man became very nervous and refused to accept the box. He told the whole story to the officer but nobody was ready to believe him. The young man was arrested, handcuffed, and sent to prison. After several months of hard struggles with his law suits, he was released. He lost a part of his business, good name and a lot of money too. He felt very ashamed for his stupid weakness and infatuation. This is indeed so true that human conduct is ever unreliable until anchored in Divine. Sri Kṛṣṇa tells Arjuna that in order to live in peace and happiness, we have to learn to live in the consciousness of the Supreme-Self and act in harmony with the voice of the Supreme-Self.

The Concept of Swadharma :

After giving a long description of Karmayoga, Sri Kṛṣṇa draws Arjuna's attention to the concept of Dharma. He declares that whenever there is a decline of Dharma and the rise of Adharma, I manifest myself in order to maintain the code of ethics so that the society can function peacefully and harmoniously. The word Dharma, which comes from the root word *dhar*—means to uphold and maintain. *Swadharma* means the code of conduct which is supported by the voice of the inner-self which guides us to perform our duties by keeping in mind the welfare of others. It is direct guidance from the source of life in us which prevails at the heart of entire creation. It is the experiential realization of the Supreme-Self. Any type of work which is performed with the awareness of the Self, becomes a source of peace for everybody, because in that is the manifestation of God Himself.

Any society where people become very materialistic, and when every person moves singlemindedly, in the pursuit of wealth, spirituality is usually pushed to the very far end. With the negligence of spiritual values people become selfish, and ignore *swadharma*. In this reference I like the words of the great educationist E.F. Schumacher, "If human vices such as greed and envy are systematically cultivated, the inevitable result is nothing less than a collapse of intelligence." When the feeling of jealousy, greed, envy and peer pressure increases in society, there comes the distortion of moral values, and decline in ethics all around. Any type of material progress and happiness which is preferred over ethics becomes another form of misery. It is the consciousness of the Divine which guides the person to live by the code of conduct upheld by Dharma. The Vedic sages have declared, "Not by the means of wealth only can a man fulfil himself. He requires other dimensions which he has to develop, and that is spiritual self."

Accepting the presence of the Divine and performing every bit of work with the guidance of God is Dharma; on the other hand, conscious separation from the Divine and living a life against the voice of the Supreme-soul is Adharma. Dharma brings people closer to each other while

Adharma disintegrates. The decline of Dharma (righteousness) starts at the individual level and gradually spreads throughout the community and nation causing a downfall of the entire human race. Decline of Dharma is the decline of morality, virtuosity and spiritual values. The decline of ethics happens due to the loss of self-respect and due to the loss of respect for God. The lack of faith in our own self is also due to lack of faith in God. When people lose their conscious touch with God, they lose touch with themselves and with everybody and everything around. People become very insensitive, selfish, and corrupt. This is what Sri Krṣṇa says — *yada yada hi dharmasya glanir bhavati bharata abhyuthanamadharmasya tadatmanam srjmyaham,* that is, whenever there is the decline of Dharma and the rise of Adharma, O' Arjuna, then I incarnate Myself.

Here Sri Krṣṇa is speaking to Arjuna as the Higher-self of each and everyone of us. The Lord incarnates Himself to enlighten people so that they can recognize their own divinity by their own efforts. The Lord incarnates to make people realize that each and every human being is an eligible candidate for Divine status. He guides people by the example of His own personal life. The God-incarnate comes down to the level of human beings, in order to educate them into graciousness of the human life. He strengthens their faith in God and also their respect for the laws of Dharma. He shows His personal compassion for people and inspires them into godliness. He helps people realize the values of Dharma. Although the Lord-incarnate can accomplish His work without manifesting Himself, but he wants human beings to develop self-respect. The God-incarnate likes His work to be accomplished through man in order to teach him about the greatness of human life.

Sri Kṛṣṇa also tells Arjuna that the world is a vast field of mixed actions. People driven by their conditioned nature choose the kind of work they like. It is the *svabhava* or the conditioned behaviour which has created the fourfold work-order in society. The word caste is self-explanatory— means the role a person assigns himself to play in his life time. Since times immemorial people have always divided themselves into four different classes, guided by their *svabhava* (innate nature). Even today we can see this division of work in almost all the developed cultures of the world. For example, the first section is the teachers, philosophers, scholars and learned people of the society; the second one is administrators, managers, leaders, soldiers; the third is businessmen, industrialists and the fourth is workers, servants and the labourers. The caste system has been based on the *svabhava,* means the inborn nature which is expressed in the type of work we choose to perform in course of life. This self-imposed classification of people in society has always helped the community in proper distribution of work. Sri Kṛṣṇa is emphasizing that each and every person is very special and it is his responsibility to explore his unique talents and make the best use of his potentials. The administration should also provide an opportunity and means for the full expression of his *svabhava,* which eventually becomes his *swadharma*—a means for self-expression, self-realization and God-realization. People everywhere follow the fourfold law of their own instinctive behaviour and perform the work accordingly. Sri Kṛṣṇa says, although it looks on the surface that 'I' created the fourfold division, or God created the fourfold work-order in society; but as a matter of fact it becomes created by itself—by the people, of the people, and for the people. People create everything for themselves forced by their conditioned behaviour.

Sri Kṛṣṇa also explains to Arjuna the triple classification of actions. He tells that life is a vast field of actions and it is important to understand what is mandatory action, prohibited action, and what is inaction—*karma, vikarma* and *akarma.* While explaining the nature of action

Sri Kṛṣṇa declares the necessity of performing prescribed duties for the sustenance of body. If a person ignores to perform these duties he creates serious problem for himself and for others. For example, the duties of day-to-day life, regarding the personal hygiene and duties towards the family, business and society. So it is our responsibility to understand the nature of our personal duty. He gives a detailed description on the meaning of the terms *karma,* *vikarma* and *akarma,* by understanding which the person becomes enlightened and his life becomes a blessing. He tells Arjuna that self-awareness is very important while doing any type of work. With self-observation one can understand clearly the nature of action and can work with clarity and precision. In general, the human behaviour more or less is like an automated machine where emotions, memories and feelings find their expression like a preprogrammed floppy-disk. There are only a few in millions who are fully aware of the nature of their work and actually like and enjoy their assigned duties.

By *vikarma* Sri Kṛṣṇa means the activity which is performed in a deluded state of mind and also the activity about which we are not even aware. In fact forbidden actions are also called *vikarma.* He explains to Arjuna:

Karmano hyapi boddhavyamca vikarmanah akarmanas ca

boddhavyam gahana karmano gatih. It means the nature of action is very intriguing; some times even the learned men and great leaders become confused in deciding between action and non-action; the right action and the forbidden action. There is a very thin line which separates the right action from the prohibited action. So it is important for us to learn to live in the consciousness of the indwelling-soul and perform all our work with the guidance of the Divine. He makes it very clear that inaction or *akarma* doesn't mean no activity at all, it is the renunciation of the desire of the fruits of action. The very term inaction is self revealing. Inaction or inaction means while doing action, the mind stays absorbed in that action. In other words, we can say living in the awareness of the Divine while performing all actions is inaction. It is the understanding of truth that every activity proceeds from the indwelling light, and every bit of work is performed by the indwelling Self. Such actions become enjoyable and benefit the individual as well as others. The person lives his life in constant communion with God and performs all work in copartnership with God.

The actions which are performed with the consciousness of the indwelling light are always the right type of actions-contrary to the actions that are undertaken in a confused state of mind. It is very important for us to train ourselves into a disciplined state of mind which seeks guidance from the inner-Self.

He also explains that it is the experiential knowledge of the Self which upgrades the quality of all actions. This knowledge comes to us from spiritual guidance and by our own wholehearted efforts. In order to make any type of spiritual progress we have to go through these four stages of spiritual advancement. The first one is 'Atma-kripa' means the grace of the individual-self, in other words the personal effort and personal decision. The second is 'Gurukripa' means the blessings of the Guru or the learned teacher. The third one is the 'Shastrakripa', means the blessed devoted study and understanding of the scriptures and the fourth is the 'Prabhukripa' means the grace of the Supreme Divinity. The proper understanding of the ancient scriptures, and the knowledge of the Self, is possible with the grace and guidance of a learned teacher.

There is an incident from the life story of Swami Dayanand Saraswati. Swamiji had read hundreds of books in search of truth. He went from one school to another in pursuit of knowledge but still felt empty and restless, until he finally approached Swami Virjananda with utmost humility and devotion. When Swami Dayanand knocked

at the door of his Guru—a voice came from inside of the
hut and said, "Who is at the door?" Swami Dayanand's
humble answer was *"yahee to jaanene aayaa hun ki main
kaun hun"*— I have come to your door to know "Who am
I? Whom do I belong"? Swami Virjanandaji heard this
answer; his heart was touched with joy for the dedicated
disciple. He accepted Dayanand for initiation instantly and
guided him into the understanding of sacred scriptures and
the yogic mysteries of Supreme-Self.

It is not only the knowledge gathered and absorbed
from books, that brings awakening in life. Wisdom comes
from the words of the other enlightened souls and from
our own inner guidance. Guru is a channel for sharing
God's power and grace. The bond of a guru and disciple
is a special bond of divine love, reverence and friendship
which generally continues from one life to another. Sri
Kṛṣṇa glorifies the purifying power of transcendental
wisdom, guidance from the spiritual teachers and tells
Arjuna: *"tad viddhi pranipatena pariprasnena sevaya
upadeksyanti te jnanam jñaninastattvadarsinah"*—means the
initiation and guidance into the knowledge of the absolute
truth is shared by the learned sages. Their scriptural
knowledge is always combined with their own experiential
knowledge of the Self. They should be approached with

reverence, humility and an attitude of sincere service. He explains that the knowledge of the Self is a blessing and it is revealed to that person only who is receptive, faithful, sincere and determined. *Sraddhavanlabhate jñanam*—means only the faithful and devoted ones attain true knowledge. Although our relationship with the Divine is primordial and perennial, but we become receptive to the grace only in proportion to the degree of our faith, willingness and determination. The word *sradha* has been pronounced in many ways. *Sradha* is the basis of all success in material as well as in spiritual life. It is the most sincere form of devotion and respect that comes from the deepest levels of consciousness. *Sradha* is like going into the most intimate and honest relationship with the Supreme-Soul, which gives strength and inner integrity.

Sri Kṛṣṇa makes it very clear that the people who are devoid of faith definitely live a very dull and restless life. Since they don't have any firm faith in God, they lack faith in others. It is noticed in the modern educated societies that most of the people live a very fearful and stressful life. The question naturally arises, 'why these people are so stressed and so insecure'? The answer is simple. They lack faith in their own-selves. Lack of faith in their own-selves is due to lack of faith in God. So in order to live in peace and harmony with others and with our own self it is very important to be devoted to God and have faith in God, and remain grounded in the nature of the Supreme-Self.

Meaning of Sannyasa :

With reference to the meaning of *sannyasa* Arjuna brings up the similar type of question as before. The human mind has the habit to program its own portfolio, in respect of hearing, speaking and ignoring etc. In general we make judgements and listen only to whatever suits us. Arjuna repeats the same type of question over and over again, because he pays attention to that only whatever he likes to hear. In fact it is so true that in moments of selective hearing, the inner wisdom is usually lost momentarily and our concentration becomes disintegrated. Arjuna is still so absorbed in his own thoughts that he is constantly missing the most valid points in the message. Besides, he has been trained as a warrior and an archer par excellence. He definitely doesn't have the desire to listen to spiritual wisdom. He still believes that the knowledge of the Supreme-Soul and spiritual philosophy is separate from day-to-day problems of daily life. He does not understand the mystery that being spiritual and being a karma yogi is indeed just two facets of the same coin. Being spiritual is to live in the awareness of the spirit—and being karma yogi is to live in yogic unity with the source of life and performing all our work in communion with the Holy Spirit. We have to be spiritual just in order to function harmoniously and peacefully. Arjuna feels confused about the conflicting statements such as the renunciation and at the same time, action in yoga. He appeals for a decisive opinion, about the 'one' which is better.

Sri Krsna knows that understanding the philosophy of Karmayoga is very difficult. He proceeds step by step. He starts with the meaning of *sannyasa* (renunciation). He tells that renunciation and the performance of actions in Yoga, both lead to the highest good; but of the two, the yoga of action is indeed superior. In general, the word *sannyasa* is related to complete renunciation of the world. Sri Krsna calls that person a perpetual *sannyasi*, who has risen above the dualities of life; who is peaceful and works with the serenity of inner peace and has the ability to make useful and harmonious choices. Such an individual is subjectively aware, alert, content, peaceful and balanced. He performs all his duties in an alignment with the source of life. He respects life as it comes with all its ups and downs of honour and dishonour, gain and loss, pleasure and pain.

He makes it very clear that renunciation from the world, without proper knowledge of Karamyoga can be really dangerous and harmful in certain respects. A person cannot become a renunciate *(sannyasi)* by merely giving up the family life or by running away from his duties out of frustration and failures. This type of *sannyasi* loses self-respect and becomes ridicule for himself and for everybody else. It is the performance of action in yoga that prepares the person for renunciation. It brings purification at various levels of awareness and infuses the spirit of sacrifice, kindness, charity and compassion. Anybody who understands the ideal of selfless action becomes pure and goes into the status of a *sannyasi* in due course of time. The gospel of selfless action makes the path of renunciation enjoyable and interesting. Karmayoga is a means for attaining the state of renunciation. Sri Krṣna glorifies the importance of devotion, dedication and unity with the Supreme-Soul which is the basis of genuine renunciation. He explains that by living in constant awareness of the Supreme, one develops an intimate relationship with the Divine. As the bond of love for God becomes stronger, the detachment and renunciation comes spontaneously.

Sri Krṣna gives the analogy of a lotus flower which blossoms beautifully above the surface of water, with its roots in the pool. The lotus looks very fresh because of its unity with the light of sun. Similarly, a Yogyukta who remains rooted in the awareness of the Self, he lives a peaceful, happy and integrated life while performing all the assigned duties of life. With the practice of living in meditative unity, a person upgrades himself to the level of Divine consciousness and then, he is helped from within to maintain his spiritual awareness under all circumstances. He tells Arjuna that the yogi is not only that person who has renounced the world and sits in a cave to meditate, but also the one who lives enthusiastically every moment of worldly life with his mind anchored in God.

Sri Kṛṣṇa also explains the philosophy of karma and destiny in detail. He says that life and everything else, is a manifestation of mixed actions. People guided by their conditioned behaviour, perform good and bad deeds; and they are punished and rewarded accordingly. As a matter of fact, between God and destiny, there is something on which every person has his control; and that is how he performs his actions. In the words of Swami Vivekananda, "Karma is the eternal assertion of human freedom". In a way, we are the creator of our own destiny. In our day-to-day life we feel that we are being pushed along by the circumstances and sometimes we blame God and others for our misfortunes. But most of our frustrations are due to our own conditioned behaviour and the lack of our conscious connection with the source of life. As a matter of fact each and every person is the maker of his own destiny and is indeed responsible for his own fortunes and misfortunes. There are some beautiful lines by Omar Khayyam, "Be careful, for the stock-in-trade of this world's market, it is the life you purchase for yourself."

Sri Kṛṣṇa makes it clear to Arjuna that living a life in the consciousness of the Supreme-Soul is like living in eternity. When the mind is settled in the awareness of the Supreme-soul, intuition is heightened, and we get in touch with our dormant *samskaras* of past lives. We develop the ability to understand our conditioned nature. The previous *samskaras* are brought to the surface of the conscious mind under direct observation. The habit of living in the awareness of the Self, brings freedom from conditioned habits and we can create our own destiny with the pure guidance of the Supreme-Self.

Sri Kṛṣṇa declares that liberation or *moksha* is not something to be achieved after departure from the world. Liberation and absolute Bliss can be experienced in our present life as well as in the life hereafter. Freedom is living in the awareness of the Divine; freedom is the acceptance of the Self, freedom is living a life free from worldly desires. Every person is essentially Divine, but because of his slavery to the conditioned inclinations, he loses his conscious relationship with the inner Divinity and lives like a prisoner in his own house. It is true that all of us need some reasonable financial security, food and shelter to live but when simple needs of day-to-day life are stretched out of proportion, they become the cause of bondage and slavery. It is the pursuit of false values, which is the cause of slavery.

There are some beautiful words written by Rabindranath Tagore where he writes about the slavery of the embodied-soul. He says, "I am ever busy building this wall all around; and as this wall goes up into the sky day by day I lose sight of my true being in its dark shadow". This is what happens to most of the people in the world. The desires of worldly enjoyments are indeed the cause of imprisonment, bondage and slavery. People consider their luxuries to be their necessities and that is why they live in bondage.

Sri Kṛṣṇa tells Arjuna that anybody who develops a conscious connection with the essentiality of his pure and unconditioned nature he is liberated even in his lifetime. He becomes very content, integrated and peaceful. He is blessed with the right intuition and perception which brings clarity of understanding and liberation in due course of time. The inner purification, renunciation and liberation— all this is an ongoing process towards self-realization and the attainment of Brahman—Nirvana, *moksha* or absolute liberation.

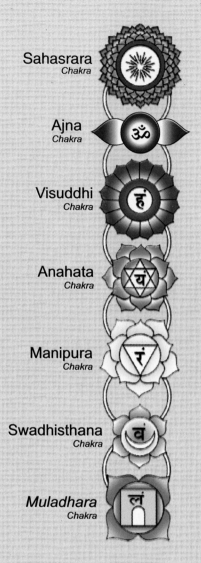

Sahasrara
Chakra

Ajna
Chakra

Visuddhi
Chakra

Anahata
Chakra

Manipura
Chakra

Swadhisthana
Chakra

Muladhara
Chakra

Eyes cannot see the Supreme being nor can words express it, nor can it be reached by other senses and cognitive faculties.
The Supreme being is only revealed in *dhyana*.
Dhyana (true meditation) is only possible when Consciousness is spiritualized by purity of knowledge of the self.

— *Mundakopnishad 3.1.8*

3

Meditation
&
As is the Macrocosm so is the Microcosm

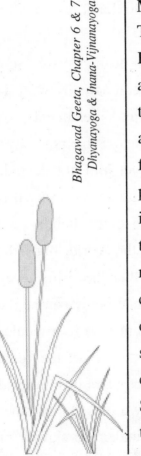

Bhagawad Geeta, Chapter 6 & 7
Dhyanayoga & Jnana-Vijnanayoga

Meditation :

The dialogue opens with words of Sri Kṛṣṇa. He repeats that renunciation and the yoga of action are essentially the same. He makes it clear that the attitude of selfless action is a means for the person, who wants to make progress in yoga; and when perfected in Karmayoga, peace within becomes the guide. A quiet mind enjoys reposing in God. Sri Kṛṣṇa makes it clear that detachment from the fruit of action comes from inner peace and silence, and inner peace and silence comes from yogic unity with the Supreme spirit. Learning to work with the guidance of the Supreme-Self is

Karmayoga and renunciation in essence. With reference to the philosophy of karma and destiny Sri Kṛṣṇa declares that the rise and fall of every person is within his own control. All of us are born with positive and negative impulses that are constantly conflicting with each other. For example, our conditioned nature tells us to enjoy everything in the material world; but while enjoying all this—some inner voice keeps reminding—Seek inner silence—seek inner enjoyment. "Go back where you belong".

The human soul being a fragment of the Cosmic Soul can rise to the status of Divine, and can actually work in a copartnership with God. As Swami Vivekananda has said, "Each soul is potentially divine." Sri Kṛṣṇa says, "Let a man lift himself by his Self; let him not degrade himself; for he himself is his own friend and he himself is his own enemy". Anybody can rise to the height of a genius and can become the glory of the world, but if he ignores the voice of the inner-self, then he drifts away from *swadharma,* and he falls. A human being can be the splendour and majesty of the world but also its ridicule.

For example, if a person remains aware of the voice of God he remains aware about the activities of mind and he definitely acts like a friend of his own self. On the other hand, when a person acts carelessly under the slavery of his conditioned behaviour ruled by the lower-self, he becomes his own enemy. The ignorant and irresponsible people blame others for their failures and misfortunes, while in reality each individual is responsible for his own life. He is indeed his own dear and reliable friend and also his own most dangerous enemy.

Sri Kṛṣṇa tells Arjuna that it is through regular practice of meditation we can purify our thoughts. Then we can become more aware of the processed information in mind and thus can improve the quality of life. Meditation means to attend to the thoughts with attention and intention. In meditation we learn to attend to ourselves by watching, observing and beholding the movements of our thoughts, ideas, and aspirations. It gives us ability and opportunity to examine ourselves and monitor the quality, quantity and direction of our thoughts. It is a systematic practice of knowing our own selves at various levels of consciousness. It is the method of exploring the inner dimensions of our personality and ultimately being introduced to the essentiality of our own nature. Regular meditation enhances intellectual abilities, intuitive powers and improves the quality of life. It gives us the ability, strength, and insight to develop a positive control over the activities of mind, and also of our lives. As we observe in general, most of us live as a poor victim of circumstances. Quite often we feel as if we are being forced to live in a certain way; we are forced to behave in a certain way; forced to think and act in a certain way—being pushed along by our conditioned habits.

In regular meditation a person is able to attend to the internal dialogue and educate himself in monitoring the movements of his thoughts and direct them in to the serenity of the self. It is a conscious detachment of attention from a specific pattern of thoughts, which we do not want to entertain. It is a shift in awareness which gives positive control over life and the ability and strength to live the type of life one desires to live—and not the one which a person is forced to live dictated by his conditioned behaviour. Meditation is the experience of conscious control over the activities of mind and the joyful experience of inner silence. It is being in touch with the centre of our being—*saheja avastha* where, we are not compelled by our egocentric habits, where we have no regrets, no expectations, no fear and we can hold on to our essential nature which is pure, peaceful and absolute bliss. It is indeed so true that daily meditation prepares us step by step for the journey within our own self and re-orients the entire personality, where our thoughts, words and deeds all blend into one homogeneous whole and life becomes relaxed and peaceful. We are blessed with inner intimacy with divine and transcendental unity with Supreme-Self in due course of time.

Regular meditation brings spontaneous psychological transformation and helps us to recover from the vicious cycle of worrying. It initiates us into more systematic, orderly thinking. It improves intellectual abilities and also improves memory, self-confidence and self-reliance because of the grace of the indweller, which is received in daily meditation session. It promotes respect and reverence for life and helps us to renounce addictive habits and compulsive behaviour. Many stubborn, age-old, conditioned habits simply disappear due to the psychological transformation that occurs in daily meditation. Self-study and self-discovery gradually eliminates confusion, physical stress and makes life relaxed joyful and peaceful. Regular meditation does strengthen the immune system and helps to eliminate emotional stress, which brings a significant improvement in general health and our relationship with others. It helps to discover how secure, healthy, wealthy we are and how we can give and share. We can give and never exhaust ourselves which is indeed the secret of relaxed relationship with others. Disciplined practice of meditation contributes a lot to overall relaxed style of living. Modern medical science has established that almost all physical ailments are closely connected with mind. With regular meditation the entire thinking faculty is brought under conscious control which gives an opportunity to understand our emotional and physical illness and also the guidance how we can help ourselves. Help and solution for all our problems, lies within us. We have to just ask for it.

We live under the false impression that healing is only in the hands of doctors and therapists and forget our own ability to help ourselves. Eventually the healing has to come from the wisdom of our own body with the proper guidance of a doctor and our own inner healer. It is indeed so true that the conscious healing capacity of mind improves miraculously by sincere practice of regular meditation. It has been experienced by doctors throughout the world that within a few days of relaxed meditation the patient's mind calms down, the tension and frustration begins to resolve, the body becomes receptive to treatment and respect for life begins to blossom. The individual is able to view the entire situation from an expanded consciousness and immediately he finds himself optimistic, enthusiastic, tolerant, relaxed and forgiving. It is really so important to be in tune with the rhythm of pure consciousness and allow ourselves to relax and experience the alert awareness in order to create peace and harmony in daily life. This is also true that with regular meditation we can improve our sleep pattern and cure insomnia—as a matter of fact, what is insomnia? It is the inability to disengage ourselves from the unnecessary flow of thoughts—inner gossip, the inner dialogue. So with meditative ability we are able to watch the flow of thoughts consciously—monitor it and direct attention into the desired channels and guide the mind into the silence of sound sleep. This is also a well established fact that with sustained practice of meditation the aging process can be controlled to some extent. This is because of daily connection with the source of life. It is like being charged with pure energy and positive vibrations regularly and renewing the flow of life. In general, the people who meditate, are peaceful, relaxed, creative, precise and live a healthy long life.

Regular meditation gives inner strength to deal more effectively with all kinds of problems in life—physical, emotional and psychological. In the silence of meditation we do act as a co-creator of our own personality. The Vedas have declared jubilantly that when a person goes beyond the boundaries of mind and body and is settled in pure consciousness of the Supreme-Self, Brahmi chetna, he is blessed with the spontaneous ability to know anything, do anything and accomplish anything. This has been expressed as *Brahma bhavati sarati*—means when settled in Brahmi chetna , the Self becomes the charioteer of our desires and intentions. That is, when a person develops the insight and ability to make changes in life for the better. Real meditation is indeed liberation from the clutches of our conditioned behaviour. It is living in bliss, where the different aspects of our personality blend into one harmonious whole.

Sri Kṛṣṇa explains step by step the procedure of going into the state of deep meditation. It is very important to learn more about the correct meditative postures. It helps us to achieve full benefits of meditation and also makes the meditation session relaxed and enjoyable. First of all, it is indeed important to find a quiet place, because in meditation when the mind is guided into the silence of the Self, even a little disturbance can distract the mind. If we are meditating inside a room, it should be properly ventilated and devoid of all strong smells. The quiet places like a forest or a mountain peak are indeed ideal, but that doesn't mean that a family man can not practice meditation. Meditation practice is possible while living at home and with family. Any quiet corner of the house is appropriate. It is also important to sit facing east or north in mediation. East for enlightenment and north for stability; besides, it brings the special advantage of alignment with the magnetic field of the earth. The most beneficial time for meditation is early sunrise and sunset-*Brahma mahurta* and *sandhya*.

Sunrise and sunset are auspicious because the quietness across the horizon is conducive to meditation and mind becomes receptive to the call of Divine.

The glory of the dawn and dusk, the time when the day and night meet has been beautifully described in Vedas. This is the time when the air is charged with spiritual energy; mind is refreshed and free from the activities of daily life; ready and receptive to the guidance of the Self. The quietness of dawn and sunset makes the meditative experience very rich and rewarding. It is also important to choose a specific spot in the house and try to practice everyday at the same spot. It works wonders. The reason is that the particular spot of meditation becomes energized with positive vibrations. So the moment we take seat, quietness begins to flow towards the goal in meditation. In order to make the meditation session relaxed and enjoyable, a comfortable cushion is recommended. It should be placed above the ground. Actually if one elevates the seat with a low cushion that helps in keeping the spine straight and also relieves pressure on the lower back. This position locks the spine immediately and aligns the neck and head automatically.

The ideal recommended posture for meditation is padmasana. Padmasana is the full lotus position. For a beginner in meditation, this posture is difficult, so it is appropriate to start with simple posture, the crossed-legs position with a cushion supporting the seat. This simple posture is called sukhasana. Another recommended posture is sidhasana which helps the spine to remain upright and makes the meditation session very productive for a long time. With daily practice we learn to move from sukhasana to sidhasana and from sidhasana to padmasana, the full lotus posture.

The recommended posture for meditation requires proper alignment of lower back, neck, shoulder, and head. This is the vertical alignment. It helps the energy to flow from the base of the spine. It creates balance at various psychic stations and helps the body to relax and enjoy inner peace. When the head, neck and the spine align vertically, the eyes can be easily concentrated on the tip of the nose, or between the eyebrows. It is at this spot between the eyes from where the breath control starts and we can actually see the light between the eyebrows.

This proper alignment of spine prepares us for the awakening of the kundalini. The Sanskrit word 'kundala' means coiled. The life force coiled up at the base of the spine is kundalini. According to Patanjali Yoga Sutra, it is at the base of spine from where seventy two thousands *nadis* (energy canals) arise and connect the entire body with the source of energy. With the proper alignment of neck, head and the lower back, the *sushumna nadi* is awakened. Along the route of *sushumna nadi* there are seven well known psychic stations called *chakras* or the junctions where the two pranic currents *pingala* (sun-teja) from the right and *ida* (moon-oja) from the left cross *sushmana nadi,* the pure spiritual energy forming a criss-cross pathway from the bottom of the spine to the top between the two eyebrows where the union of mind, body and spirit is experienced. In meditation the pranic energy (life breath) is directed to these junction points for the proper alignment of body to the source of life with intention and attention. Concentration on these psychic stations, stimulates the flow of breath through the *chakras* and activates energy depending upon the *tattva* the specific elemental quality of that psychic station. As a matter of fact each *chakra* is a switch which stimulates a specific area of the brain and generates energy to maintain proper balance in physical and psychological make-up of the body.

Within each *chakra* is a *yantra* - a geometrical symbol associated with special *mantra* for concentration. The first one is *mooladhara chakra.* The Sanskrit word for moola means the 'root' or base and the word *adhara* means the 'support' or substratum. So the word *moola adhar* means the foundation or support centre. The location of *mooladhar chakra* is in the region of perineum at the base of the spine. It is the seat of primal energy Kundalini shakti; the reservoir of all energy—physical, emotional, mental, psychic and spiritual. The *kundalini sakti* is coiled around the *svayambhu lingam* surrounded by the deep red glow of celestial light. The elemental quality is earth. The beej mantra is *lam.* In meditation, the energy from *mooladhara* is directed to travel upward through all the other stations along the *sushumna nadi* to *sahasrara* where *shakti* goes into unity with Shiva (pure consciousness).

The second psychic station along the sushumna is the *swadhisthana chakra.* The Sanskrit word *swa* means 'one's own' and *adhistana* means the 'dwelling place'. Therefore *swadhistana* means 'the dwelling place of the self'. This station is connected with the conscious and unconscious thoughts of the present and of the many previous lives. This station is the reservoir of the present and remote memories and the instinctive behaviour which relates to the survival of the species. The location of the *swadhisthana chakra* is in the region of pubic bone in front of the body. The elemental quality is water. The beej mantra is *Vam* and the vermillion divine light is visualized in meditation. The third psychic station along the *sushumna* is the *manipura chakra* located a little above the naval in the region of Solar plexus. This *chakra,* the reservoir of solar energy, is lustrous like a sparkling jewel. The elemental quality is fire and the heavenly glow is yellow. The beej mantra for meditation is *Ram*. Meditation at this point helps the individual to enhance the elemental qualities of Agni—such as purity, vitality, self assertion, dynamism and dominance. At *manipur chakra* the yogi perceives energy of the sun radiating and permeating the whole body.

The next one is the *anahata chakra*. Anahata means the unstruck sound. This psychic station is the root of all sounds. It is also known as the heart *chakra*. This psychic centre divides the body in northern and southern hemispheres. It is located between the two breasts known as the heart centre. Air is the elemental quality of this psychic station and the beej mantra is *Yam*. This centre, the *hridayakosha* is believed to be the shrine of consciousness *(jivatma)* in human body, where the green divine light arround the Bana Lingam is visualized by the meditators in deep meditation. The first Lingam as discussed earlier is *svayambulingam* at the base of the spine at *moolaadhar;* this is the second at heart *charkra* in the centre of the body. Yogis in India and mystics of other traditions guide their disciples to concentrate on this light in order to enter the higher states of consciousness. This *chakra* is the Star of David, shooting its rays all around. Spiritual experience of closeness with Divine at the shrine of heart is a very rewarding experience in meditation. It is at this centre that the person is remade spiritually, emotionally and ethically. It is the focal point of emotional and psychological maturity, spiritual intimacy, love, compassion and cosmic unity. Just below this psychic station is another centre called the Ananda Kanda, the cave of bliss, where some people create an image of their personalized deity in meditation and actually experience the presence of God. Also at this centre the meditator is blessed to visualize the celestial tree traditionally described in ancient scriptures as Kalpavriksha or kalpataru—the wish granting tree. In some of the texts on yoga the kalpavriksha is also called chintamani means the jewel of thoughts.

The fifth chakra is the *Visuddhi chakra* located in back of our throat. The Sanskrit word *Visuddhi* means purification. In meditation on *Visuddhi chakra* the individual is blessed with serenity, purity, a melodious voice, command of speech and the special ability to communicate influentially. At this psychic station we can experience the mystical Divine nectar dripping from the *binduvisarga* which gives a feeling of blissful intoxication. Ether is the elemental quality. The beej mantra is *Ham* and cerulean blue light is visualized is in mediatation.

The sixth psychic station located between the two eyebrows is known as *ajna chakra*—means command centre. In meditation on *Ajna chakra* the individual is blessed with special ability of communicating silently with other person from mind to mind. It is through this psychic station between the two eyebrows, the guru communicates with his disciples and gives him commands. There are many other names for *ajna chakra,* such as third eye, the psychic eye, *divya chakshu, jñana chakshu,* or *jñana netra* means the eye of knowledge. It is also called the eye of intuition, meditation and contemplation. Meditation at the *ajna chakra* between the two eyebrows helps the individual to experience the unity with the Supreme-Self and makes him contemplative, concentrated and intuitive. This is the personal experience of visualizing the spark of light at *Triveni* where the two psychic currents *pingala* from the right of the spine and *ida* from the left of the spine merge into *suhsmana nadi.* The meeting place of these three *nadis* (the energy canals) is also called *trikuti* or *prayaga,* the gateway that leads the individual soul into subtle realms of preliminary superconscious states. It opens the deeper layers of one's being and initiates the mind to move into unified field of pure consciousness. It is at this specific level of purified consciousness where the individual is blessed with special mystical powers known as *ashta siddhi,* such as *anima*—which means the power to become as small as one desires and also invisible.

Mahima is the ability to expand the body in any dimension.

Laghima is the power to control the weight in body, being as light as possible and to be able to fly in the air.

Garima is the power to make the body, heavy and firm, as one desires.

Prapti is the supreme ability to achieve anything in the universe.

Prakarmya is inner integrity, extraordinary will power and the ability to work in copartnership with God.

Vashitvam—Power or taming wild animals.

Ishitvam the godlike power to control everything in macrocosm as well as microcosm.

With the increased intuition we are blessed with the clear understanding of past, present and future. This specific level of self-awareness is called *Trikal Darshan*. Meditation and concentration at this specific point between the eyebrows, known as *bhrumadhya*, awaken the desire for liberation, salvation and *moksha*. The element of this *chakra* is mind. The beej mantra is holy syllable *AUM*. The divine light that surrounds the *Agna Chakra* is cool indigo blue.

The seventh centre along the *sushumna* is known as *sahasrara*. It is the seat of consciousness which holds all the other *chakras* within itself. It is like a radiant dome of celestial spectrum with heavenly glow of violet light. It is at this point the Vedic sages used to grow a long tuft of hair. The ancient *Rishis* used to comb the hair upward and role at the top of the head, to protect this special soft spot, in order to store the spiritual energy. Actually it is like a deep well from the top of the head to the *mooladhara chakra*. Only a spark of the dormant energy from the *mooladhara* can open up this entire passage along the *sushumna* and awaken the spiritualized consciousness. While meditating on *sahasrara,* the advanced meditators do experience an ecstatic trance, and occasionally enter into the unified field where *Shakti,* the divine potency, ascending from *kundalini* merges into its source *jyotirlinga,* from where it originates. This subtle joy of unity is really exhilarating and can only be understood by those who have really personally experienced it.

To enter into *sahasrara* is the culmination of yoga meditation where the *prana* and consciousness merge into one another and mind settles in the pure void of *shunya mandala.* The illusion of individual-self disappears and yogi enters into the unified field of pure consciousness— *nirvikalpa samadhi.* This experience of unity has been described as *nirvana* by Buddhist, *baqua* by Sufis, *heaven* by Christian, *ain soph* by Kabbalists; *turiya, kavalya, shoonya,* and *nirvikalpa* by the great sages in India. After the experience of unity at *jyotirlinga* the yogi lives in an expanded state of consciousness. He has the special ability to stay in union with the super consciousness as long as he likes and then descend to other *chakras* whenever he wants to. He becomes the controller of his mind and body.

Sri Kṛṣṇa tells that while sitting in an upright position, when the psychic current flows along the *sushumna nadi*, self-purification takes place at various levels of consciousness and mind feels relaxed and concentrated. While describing a yogi who has attained concentration in true sense, some methods of concentration have been also explained. There are different ways to learn concentration. For example, the concentration on sound of *Aum* helps to become familiar to the sound of internal *nada* which leads into deep meditation. The concentration on the sound of *Aum* brings back the memory of the primordial sound—*brahmanad* and helps us to recognize and experience our closeness with the Divine.

Tratak, or fixing the eyes on some external or internal object, is also a powerful method of concentration which encloses thoughts into a small circle, and the scattered attention into peaceful meditation. *Tratak* or steady gazing at an object without blinking is one of the six purification practices called *shatkriyas*. It strengthens the power of concentration, purifies the mind and body; and also improves eyesight. *Tratak* is practised by sitting absolutely still at one place and fixing the eyes on a particular symbol or the unflickering flame of a candle. Place the chosen object at eye level, about three feet away. Sit in an upright position and regulate the breathing; then start to gaze at the object without blinking. After about a minute, close the eyes and visualize the object at *ajna* or *anahat chakra* while keeping the inner gaze steady. With regular devoted practice as concentration grows deeper, extend the period of gazing with eyes open and then closed, for about an hour or more. Sri Kṛṣṇa tells Arjuna about steady gazing at *bhrumadhya*—the space between the two eyebrows and at the tip of the nose which leads the mind to focus with pinpoint accuracy and awakens *kundalini*. In the beginning just one minute of steady gazing is sufficient and can be extended with gradual practice.

Some yoga teachers highly recommend the use of *mantra* for concentration in meditation. The word *mantra* is a combination of two words *mana* and *tra*—*mana* means mind and *tra* means to liberate. "*Mana trayati iti mantra*", a word which liberates the mind is mantra. Concentration on mantra *jaap* creates corresponding awareness of the Supreme-Self and guides the mind in meditation. Concentration with breath control is also the most well-known type of meditation practice. There is a very subtle and powerful relationship between the breath and the thinking faculty. The stability of mind is closely related to the breathing pattern and the other functions of the body.

As we generally notice, sometimes when we are emotionally upset our breathing pattern becomes turbulent. So in order to make the mind and body relaxed, we have to monitor the breathing pattern. As the breathing becomes relaxed, the mind and body also become relaxed and peaceful, and concentration in meditation comes quite naturally and spontaneously. After sitting in a comfortable position with proper alignment of spine, we should pay attention to the incoming and outgoing breath—inhalation, exhalation, inhalation, exhalation. The regulated flow of breath helps in concentration and helps us to move into meditative quietness.

In yogic meditation when the mind becomes free from all types of thoughts, a specific silence is perceived. The catching up of this silence between the two thoughts, and just being there, is going into unity with the Supreme-Soul. Although in the beginning, we can stay in silence only for few seconds, but with gradual practice, as the silence extends longer and longer, the meditation period becomes long, effortless and enjoyable.

Sri Kṛṣṇa tells that each and every person is a potential candidate for going into transcendental meditation and yogic unity with the Divine, all one needs is determination and constant sincere practice. None of the spiritual teachers or a Guru can really help anybody completely. They can help to some extent for sure, but every person has to pursue the path all by himself.

Now coming back to the definition of *sannyasa* Sri Kṛṣṇa tells that the first and foremost duty of every person is to learn to live in the awareness of the soul. Unity with the silence of the Self is *Yoga*, and the practice of that yogic unity in everyday life is *sannyasa*. He tells Arjuna that a self-realized person consciously resides in Me, works through Me, talks and acts through Me.

There is an incident from the life story of Sri Ramakrishna . Once Mathur, a great devotee of Sri Ramakrishna, took him for a pilgrimage to some of the holy places of northwestern India. Their first stay was at the shrine of Shiva. In that village, Sri Ramakrishna was filled with compassion as he saw the poverty of the villagers. He told Mathur to give each one of them, at least one blanket and one good meal. When Mathur hesitated, Ramakrishna refused even to discuss it any further, and started shedding tears over the poor condition of the villagers. Finally Mathur had to agree and they went on towards Banaras. It is a fact that when a person becomes connected in yoga, he feels himself consciously being a part of the Omniscient and Omnipresent and beholds himself reflected in others. He perceives his happiness in the happiness of others and touches the entire creation with the equality of his vision.

Even after listening to the wonderful techniques of
yoga meditation, Arjuna still feels suspicious about the
stability of mind and concentration in yogic unity. He says:
O'Kṛṣṇa, mind is very powerful and stubborn. Its velocity
is faster than that of sound and it encloses in itself the
mysteries of the whole universe. I believe it is very difficult
to control it.

Sri Kṛṣṇa gives a very precise answer—'*asansayahi
mahabaho mana durnigraham calam, abhyasena tu
Kaunteya vairagyena ca grhyate*'—sure it is very difficult
to control the mind but not impossible. In general the mind
is conditioned to remain busy in those ideas and objects,
which are very dear to the person. It forms the habit of
thinking about the same thing over and over again. If we
watch our thoughts in silence, we will realize that the
thoughts of today are the repetition of yesterdays' or
thoughts rooted somewhere in the past. So at some point
we have to learn to become aware of the thoughts and
actually come out of the self-created web. The key to
freedom from the clutches of conditioned habits is to
monitor the quality, quantity and the direction of thoughts.
By constant guidance of mantra and gradual practice of
meditation, as the mind settles into the quietness of Self,
it enjoys the silence and we are liberated from the shadows

of our conditioned behaviour.

After listening to the assured answer about meditative unity in transcendence—Arjuna makes another request, to know more about the destiny of a person, who makes some efforts but falls in yoga and fails to achieve perfection. As we see in general people complain, that they have been doing mantra meditation and yoga for so long but still they have not achieved much in spiritual life, so they start losing faith.

Sri Kṛṣṇa assures Arjuna that the virtue of good work is never lost. Any one who falls in yoga and fails to achieve perfection in the present life remains eligible to achieve perfection in the life hereafter. He tells Arjuna that people live under the false impression, that the present life is a complete life and there is nothing beyond this. The present life is not complete in itself; it is just one pause in the endless journey of past and future. The present is an extension of yesterday and it is also stretching into the next day onward. Death is not the end of life. It is only a transition. According to the law of *karma* the soul keeps evolving around the *samskaras* until it finally becomes settled in the Supreme-Soul. He assures Arjuna that all the efforts of a person for self-realization and God-realization are never wasted. The pursuit goes on to his next life. He is reborn in the family of the learned people where he resumes his practice for further progress towards attainment of the final goal. He is born in a family that gives him an opportunity for suitable completion of the task which remained incomplete in the previous life. He is intuitively persuaded to take the path of self-realization and God-realization. The intuition compels him to pursue the path of yoga. He regains all the knowledge of his previous births and makes use of that for yogic unity. The progressive realization of the Supreme-self is indeed a very difficult task to accomplish in the short span of a single lifetime. Any spiritual advancement, which a person makes in one life, definitely goes with him to the next life and becomes helpful for further spiritual progress.

History is full of such illustrations. The spiritual achievement of the great sages like Sri Shankaracharya, Swami Ramakrishna Paramahamsa and Swami Vivekananda were not just the work of their present lives, they were definitely born with unmatched calibre of spiritual inheritance.

Sri Kṛṣṇa tells Arjuna that the virtue of good work whenever it is earned, goes with the person and always remains with him. Whatever spiritual progress is made in life at one point is carefully watched, recorded and preserved all along. Every person keeps picking up the scattered pieces wherever they were left in the previous lives and puts them together once again in the next life. Virtue of good work is definitely rewarded and is always helpful in yogic communion. There is no doubt about it.

Once again He glorifies the greatness of Yoga and tells Arjuna to become a devoted yogi. Yoga is like living a life totally soaked in the nature of the Divine. He tells that living a life in yogic unity is far better than all the austerities and scriptural knowledge. Scriptures are indeed a great source of information, inspiration and intellectual growth but for the real spiritual experience of the Divine, a person has to form the habit of living in yoga. A yogi's life is gracious, glorious and becomes an example for others. Sri Kṛṣṇa tells Arjuna *Tasmat yogi bhava Arjuna*— O'Arjuna, become a yogi in order to achieve the very best in human life here and in the life hereafter.

As is the Macrocosm so is the Microcosm :

After giving a long description of meditative techniques and yogic unity, Sri Kṛṣṇa draws Arjuna's attention towards the similarities in macrocosm and microcosm. He declares that the Divine and the manifestation of the Divine are not separate. Both are intimately connected. It is knowledge of the Supreme-Soul which reveals the mysteries of the universe. It is the yogic unity with the Supreme-Soul, which helps us to know everything in microcosm as well as in macrocosm. Realization of the Self means realization of all that there is—in *triloka*. A similar kind of statement has been made by Rishi Uddalaka in *Chandogya Upanishad* where he tells his son : O'Savetaketu, 'Know that, by knowing which everything else is known'.

To explain the mysteries of Absolute and the relative, Sri Kṛṣṇa has used the words *jñana, vijñana and prajñan.* The knowledge which is attained through the study of books and other resources is *jñana.* This is also called *paroksha jñana.* The *vijñana is visesha jñana* which means the experiential knowledge. *Vijñana* is also called the *aparoksha jñana.* Sri Kṛṣṇa declares that when a person takes refuge in God, he is blessed with the knowledge of real and unreal, the unmanifest and manifest Divinity. In general, people start their study from the gross to the subtle, and from matter to the spirit, means the analytical study of the relative and Absolute. In that process of scientific inquiry, it is very hard to comprehend the truth, because after some analysis, our answers become the questions. On the other hand when we move intuitively from the subtle to gross, the inner intuition guides us, helps us and the understanding of the unmanifest and manifest Divinity becomes easy. I can say from my personal experience that it is not the structured reason—it is intuition, inner wisdom which reveals the mysteries of God and His manifestations. He tells Arjuna that it is necessary to understand the proper flow of cosmic energy in macrocosm as well as in microcosm in order to realize the unity that prevails in the universe.

It is really amazing how the Supreme Lord Himself becomes everything which is manifested. God is the source of all lives, the animate and inanimate. It is His Divine potency—*shakti* which is expressing itself every where. He explains to Arjuna the separate characteristic of the manifested Divine nature and how it relates to the unmanifested. The elements that constitute the human body and the bodies of the other creatures are known as the *apara prakriti*, or the gross manifestation. Beyond the gross is the subtle nature of the Divine-*para prakriti*, which forms the essence of everything.

Sri Kṛṣṇa declares : O'Arjuna there is nothing beyond Me, and besides Me. The entire creation is threaded in Me, on Me and around Me like the strings of beads. He declares Himself to be the thread running through the entire creation. As a matter of fact the entire universe is held together by the supreme Lord Himself. As the thread running through the beads, remains unseen, so is the Supreme Lord, while holding and sustaining everything, remains unseen to the mortal eyes.

Moving from gross to subtle, from the physical world to psychological and spiritual, from the manifest divinity to unmanifest, from the unreal to real, Sri Kṛṣṇa makes it clear that omniscience of the Supreme Lord is the only truth that prevails at the heart of entire creation.

He has used the word *maya* for the manifestation of the Divine potency. The word *maya* has been used quite frequently in ancient scriptures of India. In the *Ramayana* also it is described as *go gocher jaha lagi man jai so sab maya janeo bhai*-as far as the eyes can see, it is indeed the orchestration of *maya*—the Divine potency, which originates from the triads of cosmic energy. Wrapped within the tricks and treats of *maya* people create false values for themselves, those conceal the truth which is beyond the perception of senses. In the words of Fichte, "Our seeing itself hides the object we see; our eye itself impedes our eye". For example, over-attachment to all that we have and hoping everything to remain permanent is living under the spell of *maya*. In reference to this there is an illustration in the *Mahabharata,* where *Yaksha* enquires from *Yudhishtra*—'O king! What is the greatest surprise in the world?' *Yudhishtra* answers, "Every moment people are dying and departing from the world and yet those who are alive think as they will live for ever". People usually forget that their sojourn in the world is very limited, and each and everyone has to leave, still nobody wants to accept the truth. They want to escape and avoid the topic of death. This is *maya*.

The play of *maya* is all around us. It is the spell of *maya* which conditions the unconditioned pure self into limitations; the infinite into the finite boundaries and presents the unreal to be real and permanent. Sri Krsna tells Arjuna *daivi hyesa gunamayi mama maya duratyaya mam eva ye prapadyante mayametam taranti te*—O'Arjuna the spell of *maya* is all around us and people live their lives in false values but those who are perennially anchored in Me, are definitely blessed with the spiritualized awakened intuition and are eventually liberated from the bondage of conditioned life ruled by *maya*. This is so true that when we stop following the shadows of *maya*, it vanishes and we are liberated from its tricks and treats.

With reference to the glories of devotion and worship, Sri Krsna tells Arjuna that there are four kinds of virtuous people who worship Me, the person in physical agony; the seeker of knowledge; the seeker of wealth and the man of wisdom. He appreciates every one of them. In physical or emotional pain when we seek help from God it definitely comes. An honest prayer is bound to bring recovery with special blessings. In pain and depression when a person takes refuge in God, he is connected with the source of healing. The inner wisdom helps him to develop a positive stand and respect for suffering; he learns to deal with the disease and emotional problems with a positive attitude and courage. His brief contact with the source of healing gives him the most valuable insight, which is incomparable to any external treatment. His mind and body becomes more receptive to the treatment and healing becomes very fast. In any treatment prescribed medicine and the doctor can help the patient only up to a certain point. Eventually the healing has to come from the wisdom of his own body and from his own personal attitude. This positive attitude comes from his love and respect for life; and his love and respect for life comes from his faith in his own inner-self and faith in God. The positive strength and faith which comes in short flashes, eventually helps the patient in self-realization and God-realization. I have often seen people becoming spiritual after they had a heart attack or some other health problem. There are some people who worship God for wealth and prosperity. They are also blessed with boons and bounties of life. Such type of devotion to God, although conditional, is also appreciable. The third type of devotees are the seekers of knowledge—those are blessed with special knowledge in the field they choose, in due course of time.

The fourth type of devotee is the man of wisdom, who loves God out of his love and friendship. His devotion is firm, honest, unconditional and undivided. The man of wisdom seeks an intimate relationship with God through prayers and Yoga. Sri Kṛṣṇa declares all of them to be noble and virtuous, but the man of wisdom to be very special, because he loves Him for His sake only. Loving the Self for the sake of the Self is very rare. In the words of Swami Vivekananda, "The pleasures of the Self is what the world calls religion."

Sri Kṛṣṇa concludes the conversation declaring that after going through many births the man of wisdom and true devotion is intuitively led to the subjective apprehension of Supreme Divinity and comes to the realization—"*Vasudeva sarvam iti*"—that *Vasudeva* is everything. Here *Vasudeva* stands for the Supreme consciousness which presides over cause, space and time; and is also above all. The God-realized person comprehends the fundamental essentiality; that the omniscience of the Lord is the only truth, which is at the heart of the entire creation. He takes refuge in *Vasudeva* being the highest goal and also the means to attain his goal. He rises above the limitations of mind and body and perceives himself to be a part of the Cosmic-self. His mind works in unity with the universal mind. Sri Kṛṣṇa calls this enlightened person a Mahatma which literally means a noble and virtuous soul; who stands above the rest of the crowd, and who becomes an embodiment of the Divine.

Bliss is *Brahman*, all the beings are born from Bliss, sustained by the Bliss and into the Bliss they enter and merge again.

— *Taittiriya Upnishad 3.6.1*

4

Journey of the Soul

Bhagawad Geeta, Chapter 8
Aksharabrahmayoga

The dialogue opens with a bundle of questions from Arjuna. He says, "O'Kṛṣṇa what is *Brahman?* What is *adhyatma?* What is *karma?* What is *adhibhuta?* What is *adhideva?* What is *adhiyajña?* And O' *Madhusudhana* how a person can concentrate on You at the time of death?" He makes a special request to know more about the realization of God at the time of death.

Sri Kṛṣṇa starts with the word *aksharam*—the imperishable, and eternal is the Supreme *Brahman.* The entire world is rooted in *Brahman.* As far as the eyes can see, it is indeed the manifestations of *Parabrahman,* the

Supreme-Soul. The nature of *Brahman* is inexplicable—
that is, difficult to explain in words, but during the process
of learning and austerities as we move from one perceptual
experience to another, we are able to realize the omniscience
of all-pervading infinite consciousness at the heart of the
entire creation. After the personal experience of the ultimate
reality, everything becomes self-evident, nothing remains
to be known anymore '*anando Brahmeti vyajanti*'—means
'Bliss is *Brahman*'. All the beings are born from Bliss,
sustained by the Bliss and into the Bliss they enter and
merge again.

Now, with reference to the answer of the second
question what is *adhyatma,* Sri Krsna tells that the nature
of the Self is called *adhyatma,* the path of spirituality is
also *adhyatma,* so is the science of the soul and the study
of the Self.

To the answer of the third question, what is *adhibhuta?*
Sri Krsna tells Arjuna that the elements that contribute
towards the composition of macrocosm and microcosm
are *adhibhuta*—the perishable aspect of the Divine potency.
In the entire creation, the potential dynamism, the splendour,
the glory and the charisma of the Supreme Lord can be
seen very vividly and very clearly. The entire creation is
indeed the expressive aspect of the Supreme Divinity.
Adhibhuta has been called the '*kshara bhava*' because the

material structure is made up of five elements such as ether, air, water, fire and earth. All these elements integrate and disintegrate with time and cause change in the field of relative existence. Birth and death are two expressive aspects of the eternal process of evolution. This natural course of change is called '*kshara bhava*', the perishable nature.

The creative act is karma which is the cause of everything in the world. The entire creation comes into existence from one *bhava* or one thought only, which is the primal urge, '*ek se anek*'—which means "Let me be many". This one thought *bhava* has been the creative force since the beginning of creation and is still powerful. We can see that everything in nature is spreading; forming various roots, seeds and eggs. Every seed grows into millions of similarities. Every seed has the inherent desire to become a tree, then again the tree has the inherent desire—to become a seed again. "Let me be many" gives momentum to the cycle of *samsara*. It applies to all beings and everything in macrocosm as well as in microcosm. In human body the cells are constantly dividing and giving birth to new cells. The old cells are dying and being replaced by the new ones. The Vedas have explained this beautifully : *Yatha purava macal payasc*—everything being replaced by the identical ones. The inherent desire "Let me be many," is primordial yet ever fresh all around in creation.

Sri Kṛṣṇa tells Arjuna about the mysterious cycle of creation originating from *Brahma* and going back into *Brahma*. All creatures keep revolving into the rounds of birth, death and rebirth until they realize the bondage for themselves, and make efforts for their liberation. Every individual-soul comes into existence out of compulsion, bound by the law of *karma*. Everyone in the world is moving, as if programmed in a certain software of latencies, memories, desires, *karmas* and *samskaras*. This software is called the subtle body which is the subtlest spark of *Brahma*. It is indeed the *Brahma* (the creator) who brings forth the creation.

The question may arise who is *Brahma?* The word *Brahma* is different from the word *Brahman*. The word *Brahman* or *Para-brahman* means the Supreme Soul, and the word Brahma means one of the aspects of the *Trimurti*—the *Brahma, Vishnu, and Mahesh. Brahma* is the creator of the universe. The word *Brahma* has been derived from the root word *brh*, meaning to grow and expand. *Brahma* is the cosmic subtle body (*mana, budhi, ahankara*). All thoughts, *Karmas* and *samskaras* are the creation of mind, intellect and ego. It is under the slavery of mind, intellect and ego, the soul becomes helplessly bound. Every new birth is an expression of the data programmed in our software. The entire creation is an expression of the conditioned behaviour ruled by mind, intellect and ego. The present moment is the manifestation of thoughts from yesterday and also forerunner of tomorrow. The thoughts, desires and memories which stay dormant in the deepest layers of consciousness, appear on the surface of the conscious level at the most appropriate moment and find their expression in *karmas* which keeps the wheel of creation in motion. Every individual creates a new birth for himself in accordance with the respective data programmed in his own software. Sri Kṛṣṇa has used the word "same multitude of beings"—means the consciousness moving within itself and creating millions of forms and shapes in space and time, bound by the conditioned behaviour. People check-in in this world with a baggage of past desires to be fulfilled; and also check-out with some baggage of new desires because of their additional shopping in every new life. Most of this behaviour is very unconscious and quite unknown to the individual himself. It happens compulsively and helplessly. It is our slavery to thoughts, desires and dreams that helplessly brings us back to the rounds of birth, death and rebirth over and over again. To make it clear, Sri Kṛṣṇa has used the word *avasam* which means moving helplessly pushed along by memories, desires and latencies.

There are some beautiful lines by Omar Khayyam where he writes: "And that inverted bowl we call the sky where under, crawling cooped, we live and die Lift not thy hands to it for help. For it rolls, helplessly as you and I." While describing the nature of karma and destiny, Sri Kṛṣṇa is conveying a powerful message that for liberation in the present life, one must change the inherited habits of the conditioned behaviour and false identifications. A complete understanding of the conditioned-self and the pure luminous Self is very important for freedom from the bondage of memories and *samskaras*. It is the heightened state of consciousness which helps the person to watch and monitor every little wisp of thought in programmed data of desires and memories and to rise above the binding influence of every activity in his day-to-day life. When the conditioned-self and transcendent-Self become united, the individual moves towards liberation step by step and becomes free from the bondage of birth, death and rebirth. Each new human life brings an opportunity for self-realization and liberation. Those who make efforts, regain their lost empire, but others who don't realize their slavery, remain revolving in the cycle of *samsara* which goes on and on.

The pursuit for liberation starts with a conscious shift in our thoughts. When we start questioning, "Why my life is so conditioned; why every event takes place so helplessly; why I feel bound and pushed along by the circumstances beyond my control?" The pursuit and inquiry gives us the clue of bondage and then we make efforts for liberation. Sri Kṛṣṇa makes it very clear that transcendental experience is a blessing but is surely attained by one's own efforts.

Answering Arujuna's next question—what is *adhideva?* and *adhiyajña?* Sri Kṛṣṇa says O'Arjuna in the macrocosm as well as in the microcosm all gods and goddesses are controlled by the Supreme Lord. The controller of these *daivas* is *adhidaiva*. According to ancient scriptures, there are many prayers addressed to a large number of gods and goddesses present in the body as well as in the cosmos. For example, the nine parts of DNA, says Maharishi Mahesh Yogi, have their counter parts in the nine heavenly bodies known as nine *grahas*—that include sun and moon. DNA revolves around hydrogen bonds, which corresponds to Sun god the giver of life on planet. Phosphate corresponds to Moon, cytosine to Mars, sugar to Mercury, Guanine to Jupiter, thymine to Venus, adenine to Saturn, and enzymes within the DNA to Uranus and Neptune; and also the twelve parts of the nucleotides of the DNA are connected with twelve birth signs. He further indicates that twenty-seven groups of nucleic acid found in the cell have their counterparts in the twenty-seven *naxatras* (constellations), which accounts for direct influence of the activity of these *naxatras* on the nucleic acid in the cell, especially the DNA. This is the reason why all special and daily worships in a Hindu family are performed while giving due importance to the presiding *naxatra* (constellation) the birth sign, the position of the sun, moon and other nine planets. All the five chief elements that constitute the body of the universe have been also considered gods and goddesses. The worship of these deities is performed out of appreciation. These powers are working in cooperation with each other in order to support life on the planet. Respect for the blessings of nature has been highly recommended in the holy books of almost all religions, so that human beings can learn from the sacrifice and cooperative efforts of these cosmic powers.

All the three aspects of *'Trimurti'* are the representations of the different attributes of the Supreme *Brahman*; and all these draw their power from one original source. Similarly, there are gods and goddesses in the human body those help the different organs to work in perfect cooperation with one another. For example, the presiding *devas* (gods) of eyes are the sun and the moon, the speech is *agni* (fire), the hearing is ether *(akash)*. The deva of the organ of defection is *yama*; of the reproductive organ is *prajapati* and the controller of hands and arms *is*

Indra. The presiding deva of forehead is *Shankara* and of digestion is *Vishvanara.* All these de*vas* in the body work under the direct control and power of the Supreme Divinity. There is one vital force that presides over the inner cosmos and guides the entire functioning of the body.

This work order of perfect cooperation for the sustenance of the body is called *Yajña.* The entire work order is maintained by the controller of the body, the Lord Himself. Sri Kṛṣṇa tells Arjuna, I am the *Adhiyajña* here in the body. He is trying to convince Arjuna that the Supreme-Self is indeed the essence of the entire manifestation, whether it concerns the individual body or the cosmic body. All voluntary and involuntary activities of the body are only various manifestations of the transcendental consciousness. All kinds of worships in the form of rituals and prayers are directed towards one and the only focal point, which is *Brahman.* He is not only remote from us in some supreme status beyond but he is in the body of every being, in the heart of every man, and in nature. The supreme Lord Himself becomes everything which is manifested. God is the source of all the animate and inanimate. Appropriate perception of God's manifestation is indeed the greatest achievement of spiritual life. The entire creation is rooted in God. It is His Divine potency which is expressing itself everywhere. The Lord

Himself is everything which occurs in the material, psychological and even in the spiritual realms. Although perennially established in peaceful transcendence, Lord is *Adhibhuta, Adhidaiva* and *Adhiyajña* dwelling in the bodies of all beings.

After giving answers to the six questions of Arjuna, Sri Kṛṣṇa proceeds to answer the last question in reference to the realization of God at the time of death. He tells very clearly that it is the ruling thought in mind at the time of death which guides the person into the next life. The personality of every person is determined by the quality of his thoughts. Our entire life revolves within the cycle of past, present and future. The thoughts and feeling which we experience at the present moment is the product of yesterday, and all that which we think today makes the life of tomorrow. So the highly cherished thought of our lifetime definitely becomes the ruling thought at the time of death and determines the destiny in future. The journey of the physical body ends at death, but the journey of the soul goes on. Death is like a long sleep from where one wakes up into a new life. It is a transition. As we see in our daily life, our dreams are usually the manifestation of some thoughts that flashed through the mind during that day, or somewhere in the past. Just as one thought becomes a dream exactly like that, one ruling thought leads the person into another life. Our scriptures declare *yatha mati thatha gati*—the soul goes into the thought where the mind is settled at the time of death. It is the last thought at the time of departure from body which is the culminating point of all our memories and *samskara*s.

There is a true incident from the life of some one who is still alive. There is a family in Zambia in which a little girl Reena went through some very traumatic experiences. This little girl, at the age of six, suddenly started showing an unusual behaviour. She insisted to visit a family that lived in the nearby town. The parents felt very difficult to deal with the situation; they didn't know anything about that particular family. When the little girl became hysteric about it, they consulted their family doctor who suggested fulfilling the wish of their daughter. When they were driving, the little girl of six gave directions and the address of the particular home where she wanted to go. When they reached there, she quickly jumped out of the car and dashed into the house as if she knew everything about that place. First of all she went into a room and looked at everything around as if she was searching for something very specific in mind. While she was looking at the photographs on the walls, suddenly a seven-year old boy entered that room. The moment she saw that little boy, tears rolled down her eyes. She touched him, hugged him and immediately forgot everything as to why she was even there. For her it was like coming out of a deep sleep. Both the parents felt very strange about the whole incident. When Reena's parents inquired about the mother of that seven-year old boy, they were told that the little boy's mother had died at the time of his birth. During the conversation between both the parents, it became quite clear that in her previous life, somehow, the girl Reena had been the wife of their oldest son who died in childbirth seven-years ago. It became clear that at the time of her death she was worried about her newborn baby. Although the desire to see her newborn baby remained suppressed in the deepest layers of her mind till the age of six, but slowly it started appearing in the conscious mind and ultimately became the strongest desire and she felt restless and depressed. After meeting her baby boy, the desire and anxiety was satisfied and the remote memory disappeared. The wellbeing of her newborn was indeed one of the ruling thoughts that determined her present life.

When Arjuna brings forward the question for Sri Kṛṣṇa as to how the Supreme Lord can be realized at the time of death Sri Kṛṣṇa tells that any one who leaves his body thinking of Me alone he attains My Supreme State because of his perpetual absorption in Me. This is indeed a fact that we can't meditate on God at the last minute of our departure unless we have learned to live in the consciousness of God during our lifetime. The love and devotion of God during life time educates the individual to experience the presence of the Divine at the time of death. If a person lives a life in the awareness of the Supreme Self while working in office, while eating, while talking or doing other activities of daily life, the contemplation on God comes very effortlessly at the time of death. Sri Kṛṣṇa tells Arjuna that living a life in perpetual awareness of the Divine should become a way of life. The inner divinity must become our perpetual companion, consciously present in each and every thought, word and deed. It is through the practice of *yoga* that a person can remain aligned to the essentiality of the soul and operate in the physical world through the guidance of the Supreme-soul. At the time of death it is the yogic practice which helps the person to experience the inner vision which guides him for a single minded concentration on the Supreme *Purusha*.

The dialogue becomes interesting as Sri Kṛṣṇa explains the secrets of life here and hereafter, the art of living and the art of dying. In order to experience unity with the Supreme-soul at the time of death, we have to practice mantra meditation regularly. At the time of death a person usually recollects the past memories. His entire life runs like a video tape in the mind. And that is the reason why in every religious tradition, the relatives and friends sit around the person in order to make his departure peaceful. They read prayers and hymns from the holy books. That does help but the real effort has to come from the person himself. Concentration on the incoming and outgoing breath with meditation at the special psychic stations in body makes the last minutes very easy and comfortable for the departing soul. The thought process can be brought under control only with the rhythmic flow of breathing. When the mind settles in the breath and the breath settles in the heat and the heat in the Supreme-soul, the departure of the soul from the body becomes effortless and peaceful.

Sri Kṛṣṇa mentions *agnir jyotirahah suklah sanmasa uttrayanam tatra prayata gacchanti brahma brahmavido janah*—fire, light, the day time, the moonlit fortnight, the six months of the sun's northern course, departing in that time the men of inner alignment, the knower of *Brahman* go to *Brahman*. The fire and light in fact stands for the heat in body. This path of light and fire has been called *aarchira* path in the ancient religious scriptures. At the time of death, it is surely the heat in the body which guides the life force to make an easy departure from the body. It is the heat that keeps the breath in balance and the awareness of the Lord clear and precise. When the mind is alert the yogi can direct the life-force in the desired direction.

Sri Kṛṣṇa also mentions about closing of the doors of senses and firmly confining awareness on the primordial sound of *Aum;* which guides the soul in the realms of Divine consciousness. He tells Arjuna that at the time of death, the person should focus his attention at the heart centre—*anahat chakra.* When the life force becomes settled at this psychic station it enters into the temple of the heart, and joins the *Primordial Nada,* the sound of the holy syllable '*Aum*'. From this station the person should direct the infused breath with the vibrating sound of *Aum* upward at the *Ajña chakra* at the space between the two eyebrows.

The human body is said to be the city of nine gates, two eyes, two ears, two nostrils, mouth the organs of defection and reproduction through which a person communicates with the external world. These are also called the nine doors of perception. Yet there is a tenth sense at *Ajña chakra* which leads the individual soul upwards to *sahasrara* the *jyotirlingam.* It is the gateway to liberation and *moksha.* When the life force withdraws itself from all the other nine gates of the body and moves upward, it gradually settles between the two eyebrows which helps in concentration on the sound of *Aum.* Slowly the body consciousness starts failing and the person becomes more conscious of the Supreme spirit. This is the yogic way of leaving the body.

A similar explanation has been given in *Upanishads*—

with concentration on the rhythm of breath and with the vibrating sound of holy syllable *Aum* from the heart centre, the person should direct the breath upward as the wind is blown out from a flute. Of all the one hundred and one arteries of heart, there is one which goes upward to the crown of the head—the tenth gate of the body—*brahmarandra*. Departing from this gate from the top of the head the soul is liberated. The *yogi* who is ever connected with the Lord in *yoga*, who acts in *yoga*, thinks and moves in yoga, leaves his body in the light of yoga. The inner silence at the time of death helps him to leave body with clarity of vision.

The *yogi* who lives in unity with the Supreme *Brahman*, naturally leaves his body meditating on the Supreme-Soul. He doesn't have to make special efforts for anchorage with the indwelling soul, it comes naturally and spontaneously. The person, who knows the art of living, definitely knows the art of dying. For a yogi death becomes a celebration. That is why Sri Kṛṣṇa says : *tasmat sarvesu kalesu yogayukto bhavarjuna*—O'Arjuna stay aligned in yogic unity from moment to moment. He tells Arjuna to understand the importance of yogic unity in life and learn to live in the awareness of the Divine under all circumstances. It is through the practice of yoga we can remain grounded in the essentiality of the Self and work in the world through the guidance of the Supreme-Self. It is through the practice of Yoga, we can learn to live in yogic unity and die in yogic unity with Supreme *Brahman*.

After giving some glimpses of the techniques which help the person in God-realization at the time of death Sri Kṛṣṇa draws Arjuna's attention back to the concept of *ananyabhakti* meaning undivided devotion to the Divine. Although it is important to learn and practice the various techniques of yoga meditation but these techniques become more rewarding if supported by *ananya-ceteah satatam yo mam* i.e. perpetually living in the awareness of the Self. The person, who lives a life in constant adoration of the Divine and dedicates all his work as a service to the Divine, gets liberated from the bondage of karma while living in the world. Salvation, liberation after death, does not mean anything special to him because he lives in freedom and departs from the world in freedom. For the person who holds an undivided devotion to God during his life time, meditation on the sound of *Aum* at the time of death comes as a second nature. He lives his life in harmony with the primordial *nada* and so he departs in perfect peace with the Supreme-Self. When association with the Supreme-Self becomes the joy of life and the richness of every moment, life becomes an eternal reservoir of peace and happiness.

Sri Kṛṣṇa declares that anyone who thinks of Me without deviation; who offers himself in My service with undivided attention, surely attains Me and all My love. He lives under the blessings of My blissful umbrella—always in My protection and I am always within his reach. For him the highest aspiration of life is closeness with the Divine and service to the Divine. In perpetual unity with the Supreme Lord, the individual is definitely blessed with the vision of the indwelling Divinity at the time of death and attains salvation.

Sri Kṛṣṇa has highly glorified the power of the holy syllable *Aum*. The sound of *Aum* is the whisper from the unified field of pure consciousness to itself and the entire universe is just the orchestration of that whisper. This sound from *Brahma-nada* wraps the entire creation. Everything in macrocosm as well as in microcosm is the sequential revelation of this mysterious sound which is whispering and manifesting through every molecule and every atom.

Meditation on the sound of *Aum* has been highly glorified in the Vedas. This mystic syllable is known as the root mantra—heard by Vedic sages in deep meditation at a specific level of yogic unity in transcendence. The great mother *Gayatri* has been revealed from the holy syllable *Aum* and from *Gayatri* has been revealed the knowledge of the Vedas. The sound energy of the holy syllable AUM is a connecting link to the entire universe, as well as to the deepest mysteries of the Supreme-Self.

There is a long description of sound meditation in *Samveda*. And *Yajurveda* also explains about contemplation on the sound of the holy syllable *Aum*. *Kathopanishad* declares—that *Aum* is *Parabrahm* itself and *Mundak Upanishad* describes the unity in meditation with the mystic sound of *Aum*. *Chandogya* U*panishad* opens with the declaration *Aum iti etad aksharam udgeetam upaaseeta Aum iti hrid gayanti*—singing and meditating on the sound of *Aum* as *udgeeta* exhilarates the mind and helps in going into ecstasy of Divine love. The mystic syllable *Aum* has the power to awaken within the mind the corresponding God consciousness. It prepares the mind for going into the quietness of the Self. Through constant repetition the mind gets into the habit of being absorbed in the spiritual ecstasy created by the holy syllable. Concentration and meditation on the sound of *Aum* is indeed a vehicle of spiritual illumination. It helps the person to regulate and harmonize the entire thinking faculty into a certain order. It gives the insight and ability to experience the mystic reality through a very simple and natural method. Although we can start our spiritual pursuit according to our choice with verbal prayer, hymns and yajña, but gradually we need something short and concise, brief but comprehensive in expression, which can touch the deepest layers of our consciousness, and the primordial sound meditation does it.

Concentration on the sound of *Aum* connects us to the indwelling supreme-Self as well as to the entire universe. *Brahmanad* holds within itself the totality of everything in universe. The philologists believe that all the vowels have originated from *Aum*, and have asserted that if one concentrates and repeats the vowels for a few minutes, like A E I O U, the sound of *Aum* can be heard resonating clearly. *Aum* is considered to be the source of all Sanskrit alphabets and the source of all languages. It is also believed that the basic seven sounds of music have originated from the primordial nada *Aum*. These seven basic sounds or the *swara* as described in the *Sama Veda* are—*sa re ga ma pa dha ni sa* (*do re me fa so la si do*.) The sound of '*Aum*' is difficult to capture, but the person who meditates regularly—he can capture the sound effortlessly. According to *Mandukya Upanishad, Aum* symbolizes the triads in time and space and also the three stages. 'A' for the waking stage (conscious level), 'U' describes the dream state and 'M' stands for deep sleep. Yet another theory states 'A' to be symbolic of *Vac* (word), 'U' for *Mana* (mind), 'M' for *Prana* (breath). When written in Sanskrit, there is a curved line on the top which indicates dreamless-*turiya;* when the individual-soul goes through the gap into unity with the universal-soul. This half syllable leads the meditator into silence. The dot on the curved line represents the Supreme Divinity in us. *Omkaram bindu sanyuktam nityam dhyayanti yoginam kamadam mokshadam chaiva omkaraya namo namah.* Meditating on the dot is going into the unified field which is beyond the three levels of consciousness. Meditating on the dot is going into the silence of the Self. In meditation this stage is known as *turiya.*

Three syllables also describe the three stages of evolution in the universe. 'A' stands for adimata (beginning), 'U' stands for *utkarsha* (sustenance) and 'M' stands for *mitti* (annihilation). It also describes *akara, ukara and makra* that combine together *omkara. Akara* stands for *Ishwara. Ukara* for *moolaprakriti* and *makara* for *maya shakti.* This means that everything we see in the universe is going through an evolution. It comes into existence, it is sustained for a while and then it is gone. Everything is enclosed within the grasp of the swift moving time. Meditation on the holy syllable *Aum,* helps us to get in touch with the various stages of consciousness and experience the reality of the world. The mystic syllable also stands for *Brahma, Vishnu* and *Shiva*—the cosmic cycle of creation, sustenance and destruction. The primordial sound of *Aum* is called the *Brahmanada* which holds within itself the totality of everything in the universe. It is the sound of *Aum* which can be heard with concentration in the heart centre. There are seven well known psychic stations in human body called the seven *charkas*—the junction points. These psychic stations are located along the *sushumna nadi* where the two psychic currents *ida* from the left and *pingala* from the right cross each other. In yoga meditation the awareness is guided through these stations with full consciousness to the *Anahat chakra*. 'Anahat', as the word itself explains, means unstruck sound. At this centre vibrates a celestial sound which can be heard in deep meditation. When we withdraw our attention from all external sounds of sensory organs, this primordial sound can be heard automatically. At the grossest level the sound of *nada* is more or less like the sound of humming bees—a little deeper, it can be heard more like the melody of a flute. The third sound is more like the far off ringing bells, and as the person goes deeper into the subtle layers of consciousness, the *nada* is heard like the sound of the celestial conch. Further, at the deeper levels of consciousness one hears the sound of *Vina,* and at the subtle level one can hear a specific sound, which gradually changes into a vibrating melody, and resonates like the sound of *Aum*.

Meditation on the sound of *Aum* is very difficult, but

with proper alignment of mind, body and spirit, one perceives the melody quite spontaneously and effortlessly. Every person in the world is born with the sound of primordial *nada* which vibrates from the *anahat chakra* at the heart centre. The little infants know instinctively how to listen and enjoy the blissful sound. As we see quite often, they smile in their deep sleep because of their inner unity with the Self. A little baby knows how to recognize the primordial sound; but as we grow old, the external sounds overcrowd our mind. When the mind becomes involved in the external sounds, it almost forgets about the inner nada and we lose touch with the inner sound and inner serenity. The concentration on the sound brings back the memory of the primordial sound '*Aum*' and helps us to recognize and experience our closeness with the Divine.

The simple practice of repeating the holy syllable *Aum* and remaining aware of the sound is in itself an austerity which purifies the mind and makes us receptive to the voice of God. Meditation on the sound of Aum creates alignment with the Supreme reality from where the flow of life receives guidance. Sound meditation is not just a religious practice. It is certainly a necessity of life. It helps us to live in harmony with the voice of the indwelling-Self, with others in society and with nature.

Sri Kṛṣṇa makes it clear to Arjuna that the person

who lives his life in harmony with the *primordial nada*, definitely departs in perfect peace with the *primordial Self.* When the yogic unity with the Supreme-Self becomes the joy of life and the richness of every moment, the life becomes a celebration. The yogi knows how to celebrate life and death as well.

The universe emerges out of wholeness, it is sustained by the wholeness and into wholeness it goes back again.

— Upnishad

5

The Experiential Knowledge of the Self, Omniscience of God & Unity with the Cosmic-Self

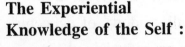

Bhagawad Geeta, Chapter 9, 10 & 11
Rajavidya-Rajaguhyayoga, Vibhutiyoga & Vishvarupadarsanayoga

The Experiential Knowledge of the Self :

The dialogue opens with the words of Sri Kṛṣṇa. He tells Arjuna that the royal science, the royal secret and the experiential knowledge of the Supreme-Soul gets revealed with pure unconditional love, and sincere undivided devotion. Sri Kṛṣṇa makes it clear that for understanding the mysteries of spiritual knowledge, one doesn't have to have much prerequisite in philosophy and religion. The knowledge of the Supreme Divinity is inherently present in all of us; it becomes revealed, when the individual becomes aligned with the source of life; remains aware of the voice of the

Supreme Divinity and follows the guidance of the Higher-Self with love, innocence and honest devotion. Sri Kṛṣṇa is emphasizing the doctrine of enlightenment and God-realization through faith, devotion, and surrender in God. He upholds the path of devotion to be the noblest and highly rewarding in spiritual journey. It has been called the Supreme purifier because it is the fulfilment in itself and also a means for increased fulfilment at the same time. It removes all shadows of egocentric behaviour from the heart of the individual in the process itself. It is indeed true that anybody who is settled in devotional services of God is guided spontaneously to a specific height of spiritual illumination where all inner conflicts are dissolved, the impurities of mind and body are washed and love for God blossoms. Literate or illiterate, ignorant or enlightened, rich or poor, man or woman, every one can follow the royal path of devotion with equal benefits. Sometime it happens that intellectuals—the so-called learned and well read people fail to accept the phenomenal power of something which is simple and within the access of every one.

It may sound odd that love of God comes simply and quickly to those who approach Him with undivided devotion and do not involve themselves in egoistic reasoning. I like what Barbara De Angelis says in her essay "An Invitation to God": "If you sincerely pray to experience God's presence into your life, it will come. The universe abhors a vacuum; if you create an opening, God will answer you. And remember, what you hear is the God within you, your own self. It's been waiting for the invitation. Once you have offered that invitation, it is important to create opportunities for the invitation to be answered—moments when you are open to feeling God reveal itself within you". She further says : "another important practice is to begin connecting with other people on a conscious spiritual path. The fellowship of like minded people is a magnet that attracts grace. When you're around people who are committed to spiritual awakening you begin resonating at the same level. Finally, watch for God coming to you disguised in different forms. God expresses itself through everything in creation". Devotional love of God keeps the person in alignment with the Higher-Self and reinforces the mind to remain settled in yogic unity at a specific purified level of consciousness. The phenomenal power of undivided devotion nurtured by sincere love of God at the subconscious level of awareness always remains with the person, no matter where he is and whatever he is doing. It keeps collecting and uniting the disintegrated energy back to its source and keeps the awareness and intimacy of the Supreme Lord conscious and alive. It helps the person to be more and more receptive to the guidance of the Higher-Self and live in harmony with the rhythms of the universe. The subtle joy of the devotional services to God cannot be explained in words—yet something which radiates from it, from moment to moment, is perceived by the devotee himself and by others around him. The blessed experience of its mesmeric touch is totally inexplicable.

Blessed are those who constantly live in the consciousness of the Divine with love and devotion—they are definitely liberated from impurities of mind and attain salvation in due course of time. That is why Sri Kṛṣṇa glorifies the path of devotion to be the noblest and the most rewarding, and declares that those who overlook the subtle power of devotional services to the Divine, and take pride in the structural explanations with tough and dry reason only, generally remain deprived of the true experiential knowledge of the Self. He makes it clear that it is good to read the religious scriptures in order to gain the basic knowledge of how to be in touch with our own inner-self and consciously live by the grace from moment to moment; but the trap is that frequently people become so involved in scriptural knowledge and egoistic explanations that they forget the real goal in spiritual journey which is inner enlightenment and self-realization. Some time even the great scholars of religion and philosophy remain deprived of the subjective apprehension of the Supreme-Soul; because only bookish knowledge is not enough for the first-hand experience of inner Divinity. Even the knowers of the *Vedas* and the great scholars have to learn to live in the consciousness of Divine for the spiritual intimacy with the indwelling-self. They have to engage themselves in loving service of God in order to experience the closeness with the source of life. He tells Arjuna that each and every one of us can find a personal relationship with God. It does require sincere love, willingness, devotion, discipline, commitment and complete surrender with an honest desire to be accepted in service. It is an exquisite experience in which the transcendental experience of closeness with Divine becomes a part of every day life and grace is experienced at every little step.

Even while speaking about the gospel of Karmayoga Lord Kṛṣṇa emphasizes the necessity of true devotion, contemplation and unconditional love of God because action has to be charged with undivided devotion for peace, success and serenity in life. Here the yoga of action, the yoga of knowledge and the yoga of devotion are graciously blended in the holy formula—Learn to live in the consciousness of God and make yourself available to the service of God.

It reminds me of some beautiful lines from *Gitanjali*

by Rabindranath Tagore "When thou commandest me to sing it seems that my heart would break with pride; and I look to thy face, and tears come to my eyes. All that is harsh and dissonant in my life melts into one sweet harmony—and my adoration spreads wings like a glad bird on its flight across the sea". He further says : "keep me at your door ever attending to your wishes and let me go about in your kingdom accepting your call. O'Life of my life, I shall ever try to keep my body pure, knowing that thy living touch is upon all my limbs. I shall ever try to drive all evils away from my heart and keep my love in flower, knowing that thou hast thy seat in the inmost shrine of my heart. And it shall be my endeavour to reveal thee in my actions, knowing it is thy power gives me strength to act".

Sri Kṛṣṇa declares *'Ananyash chintayantomam ye janah paryupasate tesam nityabhiyuktanam yoga-ksemam vahamyaham'* that the people who worship Me alone with undivided devotion, ever united in thought with Me, I assure them full security and personally take care of them. These words of assurance from Sri Kṛṣṇa have touched the hearts of millions around the world. *Ananya-bhava* literally means—total surrender in God with sincere, honest devotion and the attitude of service. Perpetual unity with undivided faith and profound reverence is what explains *nityabhiyuktanam.*

It is living in the consciousness of God with undivided devotion, love and trust. Sri Kṛṣṇa assures that anybody who takes refuge in Me I personally take care of that person. It is a fact that with sincere surrender to God the Lord's grace enters into our life in different ways and His presence is perceived. History is full of many miracles which have come across the lives of sincere devotees. The story 'Footprints' is a great example and the story goes : one night a man had a dream that he was walking along the beach with the Lord. Across the sky he saw some incidents from his life. For each occasion, he noticed two sets of footprints on the sand; one belonging to him, and the other to the Lord. When the last scene of his life flashed before him, he looked back at the footprints in the sand and he noticed that quite often along the path of his life there was only one set of footprints. He also noticed that it happened at the most difficult time of his life. This really bothered him and he questioned the Lord about it. "O'Lord, you had told me that the moment I surrendered in you; you would walk with me all the way. But I have noticed that during the most difficult time of my life, there is only one set of footprints. I don't understand, why, when I needed you most, you would leave me alone like this". The Lord replied, "My child, I love you and I would never leave you alone. During your times of trial and suffering, when you see only one set of footprints, I carried you on my back". It is true, that when and where we give up, God takes hold of us with complete assurance. When we surrender to God with faith and acceptance every experience of life becomes rewarding. We learn at every step something new and better. The unconscious relationship with the Lord becomes more and more conscious, real and alive. The conceptual reality becomes experiential and subjective. This reminds me of some beautiful lines by Howard Thurman: "Whence comes this power which seems to be the point of referral for all experiences and the essence of all meanings? No created thing, no single unit of life can be the source of such fullness and completeness. For in the experience itself, a man is caught and held by something so much more than he can ever think or be that, there is but one word by which its meaning can be encompassed—God". Sri Kṛṣṇa suggests to the entire mankind to develop a strong faith in God and purify the heart with faith and devotional services. He assures that the devotee may forget sometime to take care of what he has, but the Lord Himself looks through his interest and makes sure that everything of His devotee is secure and in perfect order.

With reference to power of prayer and efforts of seeking oneness with the Supreme-Soul, Lord Kṛṣṇa draws

Arjuna's attention to various types of rituals described in ancient scriptures. These rituals are meant to be performed to live a balanced, prosperous and blissful life on earth and attain salvation in due course of time. Religious services should be performed out of love and appreciation for the Supreme Divinity, and also for self-purification. Sri Krsna tells Arjuna that although people worship many different forms of gods and goddesses but in reality, their offering is made to the one and the only Supreme Power manifested through different forms and names. These people fail to recognize the omniscience of the Lord and remain busy in receiving transitory boons and bounties. They eventually fall from the real purpose of human life which is God-realization and Self-realization.

On the other hand, the individuals who are ever united with the Supreme-Self, gradually rise above the tricks and treats of *maya*; from *jivatma* they rise to the heights of *Mahatma* which means a great soul. They are always living in God; walking with God and working with God. Their each word comes from the depths of their love and devotion for God. The chanting of the Lord's holy name is always on their lips, and the contentment of inner fulfilment reflects through their words. They are steadfast in their vows, and are perpetually striving for the experiential intimacy with the Divine. Gathering with other enlightened devotees to pray and worship becomes their favourite past time, their entertainment and enjoyment. They are very receptive and open to the inner voice and the silent messages of Grace in the activities of their day-to-day life. These devotees of the Lord are very sensitive to the needs of other people and are always seeking opportunities to serve God and humanity. For these men of wisdom, duality of form and shape disappears and they live in constant unity with the Lord. They remain deeply grounded in the awareness of the Divine and also experience the Lord reflected through others. They worship the Absolute Lord as one, undivided and pure consciousness.

He tells Arjuna that in the middle of manifested diversity in the world, a person should always remain conscious of the Absolute Reality as the substratum of creation. Living a life in the consciousness of that one power, which reflects through everything and every body is really understanding God in essence. I like these words of Rabindranath Tagore from *Gitanjali,* "Through birth and death, in this world or in others, wherever Thou leadest me, it is Thou, the same one companion of my endless life; who ever linkest my heart with bonds of joy to the unfamiliar. When one knows Thee, then alien there is none, then no door is shut, Oh grant me my prayer, that I may never lose the bliss of Thy touch, of the One in the play of many."

In the description of ritualistic offerings and devotional services, Sri Krsna makes it clear that a person doesn't have to be rich, or learned or well known to become a devotee of the Divine. Supreme Lord cares for *bhavana* (honesty of thought) and loving devotion more than anything else. He tells Arjuna *patram, pushpam, phalam, toyam yo me bhaktya prayacchati tadaham bhaktyupahrtam asnami pryatamanah*—means that when the devotee offers a leaf, flower, fruit or even water with sincere devotion I accept the offering with great joy. He assures that the one who offers the most expensive bouquet of flowers is dear to Me, and also the one who offers merely some leaves and water is very dear to Me. The one who offers expensive pudding is dear to Me and also the one who offers a piece of bread is very dear to Me; as long as the offering is made with sincere love and devotion. It is indeed the dedicated feeling, the innocence and honesty of thought which counts the most in worship. The most cherished and desirable offering which the Lord wants from us is our perpetual conscious unity with the Supreme-Soul. Each and every activity should be centred in the consciousness of the Divine and the entire life should become a perpetual worship of the Divine. He declares that instead of marking a special time for formal prayer and meditation—just learn to live in God celebrating his presence from moment to moment. Make every activity a sacred spiritual experience. When service for the Lord becomes a way of life, love for the Lord blossoms and life becomes a blessing. This is the secret of spiritual awakening, self-realization and God-realization. Let God remain consciously present in all our thoughts, words and deeds.

Sri Kṛṣṇa glorifies loving devotion because that is something within the reach of every one. To love is a natural instinct. Love for God initiates the person into a close friendship with God and an intimate relationship with God. In close intimacy with the Divine we become more and more appreciative of the beauty and blessings in everyday life and experience a close communion with Divine in almost all activities of daily life. We begin to perceive and understand that God is all around us—working through us and working with us.

The process of spiritual progress is easy and within the reach of every one. There is nothing new to learn because every person is born with this natural instinct of love and devotion. Our practice is a shift in awareness— it is coming out of a certain type of life-frame and stepping into another one in which we open our eyes, simply look around and feel blessed. Sri Kṛṣṇa has been repeatedly trying to enlighten Arjuna about his own divine potential, for him to act enthusiastically, effortlessly and skilfully. It is indeed important for Arjuna to realize and experience the power of his own inner resources. Arjuna has to experience that he exists in God and all his activities are being carried on with the help of the power within. He has to overcome his egocentric limited individuality and work in an alignment with the Supreme-soul. Arjuna has to understand the indwelling God as the true essence of life and act consciously from the source within. Man is created, nourished and sustained by the Supreme-self but, unfortunately, still remains unaware of the Lord's presence within. He lives in his own limited identity, created from his own limited egocentric point of view.

The soul's identification with the body is very deep-rooted and is very difficult to erase. This separate limited identification of the human-soul is the cause of all fears and insecurities in life. Sri Krsna knows that Arjuna will cooperate enthusiastically, skilfully, peacefully, and harmoniously only when he is blessed with the experiential knowledge of his own essentiality and perceives his individual-self to be a perennial fragment of the Universal-self. Arjuna has to understand and experience the truth that he is indeed a fragment of the Supreme-power; and a very unique manifestation of the Lord Himself. It is only after the personal experience of his connectedness with the cosmic-Self, Arjuna will intelligently cooperate in all respects. It is only after self-actualization that he will feel more like an instrument in the hands of the Divine power.

The moment a person consciously perceives the presence of inner Divinity, and feels himself a part of the ever renewing current, his life style changes instantly. His insecurities and fears are washed away with inner enlightenment. He becomes receptive to the voice of God and learns to live in the renewed concept of reality. His capacity to work becomes enormous and he works in perfect harmony with *swadharma*. His vision becomes one-pointed and his purpose of life becomes clear to him.

Omniscience of God :

In description of the omniscience of the Supreme-soul Sri Kṛṣṇa says, "O'Arjuna ! Listen carefully to my words. I am going to tell you something very special because you are dear to Me". He knows that in order to experience the omniscience of the Lord, it is necessary for Arjuna to understand the various attributes of the Divine.

The reservoir of Divine energy is all around us. We make use of this energy by our own choice and inclination. Sri Kṛṣṇa draws Arjuna's attention towards the unity in diversity as seen in the universe. Everything is the manifestation of Divine potency.

The primordial power of the Supreme can be seen evolving itself into innumerable varieties. The word *vibhuti* stands for magnificence in several different ways. *Vi* stands for *vishesha* means special and '*bhut*' means being. *Vi* + *bhu* means appear, expand, and manifest. The entire universe is an expression of the power and the majesty of the creator. Sri Krsna the knower of human psychology understands the difficulty of Arjuna. He knows that just factual knowledge is not enough for proper understanding of truth; it has to be a subjective experience. He knows that there is a process which helps in comprehending the mysteries of the Divine. There is a method that can help us to re-group our thinking faculty into a pure and new image. That's why He initiates Arjuna into loving devotion for the Supreme-Self. With loving devotion the person moves step by step into new dimensions of self-awareness and personal comprehension of the Ultimate Truth.

Once devotion is aroused with a convinced understanding, the person remains constantly aware of the eternal truth in the middle of everything else. Here Sri Krsna has used the compound word *anukampartham* which means out of My compassion and special love I eliminate the ignorance of My devotees and enlighten them with inner knowledge. When my devotees come closer to Me, I help them in yogic unity and strengthen their faith by taking care of their personal needs and by providing them personal security.

Sri Kṛṣṇa declares, "I help them to light the luminous lamp of wisdom from their own inherent light." The expression *atmabhavastho* explains the great secret of His message about the experience of the presence of Divine from the innermost levels of our own consciousness. This experiential unity comes as a grace of the Divine and opens new dimensions of self-understanding and God-realization. *Atmabodhastha* is inner awakening. When the mind becomes settled in yogic unity, the light of Self is perceived in flashes. It illuminates everything and gives utmost clarity of vision. This wisdom is the perceptual knowledge of the indwelling soul. It comes in the form of divine grace and blessing. It is the heightened capacity of self-understanding which opens the hidden horizons of the Supreme's domain, in the microcosm as well as in the macrocosm.

Accepting the presence of the Divine is the initial step, which is strengthened by accepting the consciousness of the presence of the Lord through the experiential knowledge of the Self. It is the perceptual experience that brings transformation in the attitude of acceptance. The Supreme Lord, who is the substratum of the entire existence, becomes revealed only when sufficient efforts are made by the individual himself. The moment his mind becomes receptive to the silent call of the Divine, the subjective experience of the indwelling Lord becomes real and experiential. There is no doubt about it. This is when the intimacy with the Divine becomes a joy of life—this is when the perceptual experience becomes a personal reality. This reminds me some beautiful lines written by Rabindranath Tagore —"I will utter your name, sitting alone among the shadows of my silent thoughts.

I will utter it without words; I will utter it without purpose.

For I am like a child that calls its mother a hundred times, glad that it can say Mother".

The most important step in the process of God-realization is to wait with willingness, faith and confidence, and to synchronize thoughts, feelings and actions in the appropriate direction. It is indeed true that anybody who starts his spiritual journey with an attitude of undivided devotion; for him help comes from within his own resources and the realization of the indwelling Lord happens spontaneously.

The dialogue becomes interesting when Arjuna expresses his desire to know more about the attributes of Divine. Although he understands the omniscience of the Lord, but still he wants to know more about the mystery of unity in diversity. Arjuna makes an appeal for a clear, detailed explanation of the various significant manifestations. He feels the necessity to become introduced with the attributes which can spontaneously help him to maintain his perpetual unity with the Lord. In order to recognize the presence of the Supreme, to stay aligned with the essence of life in macrocosm and microcosm, to live a life totally absorbed in the devotion of the Supreme, in constant remembrance of the Lord, it is indeed necessary to know more in full details about the magnificence of the Supreme.

Sri Kṛṣṇa opens the conversation with words : *aham atma Gudakesa sarvabhutasayasthitah ahamadis ca mdhyam ca bhutanamanta eva ca* "O'Arjuna, I am the indwelling soul, seated in the hearts of all beings; I am the beginning, the middle as well as the end of all beings". Sri Kṛṣṇa tells Arjuna that I am *Samaveda* among the *Vedas*. There are four *Vedas*—*Rigveda, Yajurveda, Samaveda* and *Atharvaveda*. As the main theme of *Rigveda* is knowledge, so is sincere devotion for God of *Samaveda*, in other words *upasana*. The hymns of *Samaveda* are used in devotional music and also for proper knowledge of *swara*. There is a very famous hymn of *Rigveda*—*"Ekam sad vipra bahudha vadanti"*. The Supreme Lord is one, but He is called by various names.

Sri Kṛṣṇa declares that "I am the consciousness in the

living beings and *Sankara* among the eleven *Rudras.*" The consciousness in the body is called *Shiva.* When *Shiva* leaves the body, it is declared as *shava.* The *shava* is a Sanskrit word that stands for the dead body. So the consciousness in the body is *Shiva* or *Shankara.* It is the indwelling light of the Supreme-soul which sustains and maintains order in the body—when the Divine light leaves the body the individual light goes into cosmic light. A spark merging into the wholeness of the Divine radiance which has been beautifully explained in Gurugranth Sahib— *jyon jala men jala aye khatana, tyon jyoti san jyoti samana.*

Sri Kṛṣṇa says : Among the high-peaked mountains I am the *meru*—*meru* is believed to be the axis—the centre of the universe. The *Puranas* declare that on the top of this golden mountain is the seat of the Supreme Lord.

This mythological mountain peak is symbolic description of the spinal cord in the human body, the golden peak represents the *Jyothirlingam;* the seat of the Divine. Along the spinal cord in human body there are various psychic stations through which the life-force moves. In yogic meditation when this energy is consciously controlled and directed upward, it brings purification. Moving towards the peak of the mountain at the top of the head is usually the goal in yogic contemplation. The great yogins do experience the ecstatic trance through alignment and occasionally enter into the realm of Divine light where *shakti,* the divine potency, ascending from *kundalini* merges into its source *jyotirlinga,* from where it originated. This subtle experience of inner unity has been expressed by mystics throughout the world in their own unique way.

Once again Sri Krsna glorifies the holy syllable *Aum* and tells Arjuna : *pranava sarva vedhesu,* that I am the Holy syllable *Aum* in the *Vedas. Pranava* means which pervades at the heart of entire creation and is ever renewing. *Pranava* also means which runs through *prana*—the life breath. *Pranava* is a composition of sixteen *matras—akara-ukara-makara-ardhmatra-nada-bindu-kaal-kalaateeta-shanti-shanti-aateeta-unmani-manonmani-puri-madhyama-pasayanti-para.*

When we meditate on the sound of *Aum,* the Holy syllable, each one of these gives different vibrations and helps us in full concentration on the primordial *nada.* It is the realization of the Supreme-Self from form and shape into the formless reality which is beyond cause, space and time. The sound energy of the holy syllable *Aum* is indeed a connecting link to the cosmos as well as to the deepest mysteries of the Self. Sri Krsna declares the Holy *Aum* to be His attribute.

Also Sri Krsna tells Arjuna that among the different forms of worship "I am the *Jaap-yajña*". The word *jaap* stands for silent repetition of the Divine name. The mantra *jaap* is a vehicle of spiritual illumination in the form of God-realization and self-realization. It helps us to live in the light of pure awareness. It strengthens our unity with the Supreme-self. *Mantra jaap* means storing and restoring of a specific thought. Repeating mantra is like printing the impressions of a group of words, into the deepest layers of our consciousness. *Mantra jaap* contains within its words a certain type of energy which replaces the old memory with the new one and brings a shift in awareness. I like what Swami Tapasyananda used to say, "*Mantra* is something more than a prayer. It is in itself a word of power. It is a thought-movement vehicle in sound and words". Sincere repetition of mantra leads the aspirant to the specific heights of spiritual illumination where all the inner conflicts are dissolved and the complexities of mind are washed away. It helps the person to regulate, harmonize and bring the entire thinking faculty into a certain order. *Mantra jaap* strengthens our unity with the indwelling-self, and makes us aware of the power, which is the essence of the universe and how we can learn to be responsive to it. It helps us to live in the light of pure awareness and accelerates our day-to-day emotions to the journey of self-purification and self-realization.

Silent *jaap* is like being in constant communion with

God and working in a copartnership with God. The habit
of silent *jaap* sets the whole life in tune. It helps us to
experience the essence of something which is real and yet
waiting to be revealed; something so close to our heart, yet
seems so far off. A mind settled in the essential nature of
the Self becomes very peaceful and radiates inner peace
all around. Sri Kṛṣṇa tells Arjuna that among the *Vedic
chhandas*—(metres) I am *Gayatri*. There are about 24000
hymns in the four *Vedas*. The essence of all those have
been combined into 24 syllables called *Gayatri*. Atri rishi
was the great sage who sang it for the first time in the
most melodious tune since then it has been called *Gayatri*.
Our Vedas declare *gayante, trayante, yesye sa Gayatri*.
The glory of *Gayatri* has been described throughout the
Vedic literature. Meditation with the chants of *Gayatri*
connects us to the Supreme Lord the source of everything
in manifestation.

The recitation of the first three words, *bhur, bhuvah,*
and *swah*, connects the individual to all the three levels of
consciousness. These three levels are physical,
psychological and spiritual. *Bhur* symbolizes the physical
body composed of five elements namely earth, water, air,
ether and energy. In prayer the request is made for complete
harmony and support of the cosmic forces. The word
bhuvah stands for thought process as a controller of astral

body or the inner nature. *Swa* stands for the indwelling light the Supreme-Self. *Gayatri jaap* brings harmony at all the three levels of consciousness. It keeps electrifying thoughts with spiritual power. It purifies thoughts, speech and action. In prayer with *Gayatri* mantra the aspirant calls upon the divine mother—*savitur* for inner enlightenment, clarity of vision, purity of mind and intellect, precision of thoughts, inner integrity and right guidance into the activities of daily life. According to *Vedic* tradition *Gayatri* mantra is taught as the first prayer to the child, for proper alignment at the physical, psychological and spiritual levels of awareness.

Sri Kṛṣṇa concludes the description of His attributes saying : *vistavhyahamidam krtsnam ekansena sthito jagat*— "O' Arjuna I exist supporting the whole universe with the single fragment of Myself". The attributes of the Lord are surely infinite and very difficult to comprehend. *Prabhu ananta prabhu ki leela ananta.*

As a matter of fact, the entire universe is being held together by a small fraction of the Lord's yogic power. The Divine potency is indeed holding everything together and also reflecting through everything. I like what Swami Chidbhavanananda used to say, "Lord is expressing Himself. Whatever catches our imagination, draws our attention, sends us into raptures and infuses bliss into us that is none but the glory of the God." It is indeed difficult to comprehend the infinitude of the supreme; the human understanding can catch only a small fraction of it, so it is just enough to remember that the Lord is everything. In fact any type of particular glory, achievement, name or fame that comes to us should be considered to be the magnificence of the Divine glory. We should never get mislead by the masks and should learn to appreciate the splendour of the Divine behind all types of veils. This attitude of seeing the Lord's opulence and majesty in everything keeps us perpetually connected with the indwelling-self and strengthens our closeness with the Supreme-Self. It initiates us in recognizing the expression of divine grace in every bit of activity that is special and particular. We should always remember that whatever is expressed as unique and special in the form of learning, austerity, virtue, beauty, valour and victory, splendour and glory, mighty and meritorious, knowledge and intelligence, wisdom and intuition etc. presents itself as the attribute of Supreme Lord. This is the truth that needs to be accepted and recognized in order to prepare the mind for contemplation and yogic communication.

Unity with the Cosmic-Self :

After listening in detail about the attributes of the Divine, Arjuna makes another request. He says *'Manyase yadi tac chakyam maya drastumiti Prabho'*—O'Kṛṣṇa if you think, I am worthy of receiving your special blessing, please bless me with your Divine vision. In *Vishwarup Darshan* or vision of cosmic unity, the person is awakened into a specific field of super-consciousness in which his limited individual-self goes into unity with the cosmic-Self. It is like entering into the unified field of consciousness and catching the first hand experience of the Lord's magnificence, infinity and cosmic unity. It is like going into a specific level of awareness where 'I-Ness' is dissolved and the person feels totally dedicated to the will of God. Cosmic vision is a special blessing of the Divine. In order to realize one's own immortality and comprehend the concept of one's essentiality, the person has to move into the subtlest levels of consciousness, where all diversities merge into unity. The experience of the Divine vision is going into increased awareness of the mind, and looking at everything through the eyes of the cosmic mind.

The vision of cosmic unity gives a special ability to freeze time in present and perceive the past, present and future all together. Sri Kṛṣṇa knows that in order to understand and control the flow of time the person has to experience the unity with the cosmic-Self which is beyond the limitations of time and space. Divine vision is to be awakened to a specific level of awareness and to be in touch with present, the past as well as the future. It is a threefold experience all at once. It is quite similar to the type of experience in which a person standing on the top of the mountain can see everything on the top, in front and also behind, which has remained hidden earlier. Vision of the three in one is what the scriptures call as *Trikal Darshan*. Sri Kṛṣṇa the knower of human psychology knows very well that freezing past, present and future into one, will help Arjuna to see into the distant future and calculate the proper strategy for the situation at hand. When Arjuna looks at the cosmic body of the Lord he feels overwhelmed with amazement and thrilled with joy at the most blessed sight of the Supreme. The word *'Ekastham'*—means centred in the cosmic body. Arjuna looks at the universal body as 'One' unified field into which everything dissolves eventually. He beholds the cosmic body enclosing the entire creation in one unit. The cosmic vision gives Arjuna an opportunity to understand the relativity of time and that which is beyond the concept of cause, space, time. He feels exhilarated and starts singing the glories of the Lord—out of his love and devotion. The expression *pranamyam sirasa devam* literally means I salute and bow to the Supreme Divinity in You. He says O' Lord you are *anantah*—beyond the boundaries of time, space and cause. You are the God of gods, the abode of the entire universe.

Arjuna goes into Holy Communion with the Lord and feels totally blessed. The intimacy of Arjuna, reflects the primordial relationship of *Nara* and *Narayana*—the Supreme-Soul and the individual-soul. Arjuna sings the glories of the Lord with profound love and devotion. His words definitely express the purity of relationship which lies between the Lord and His genuine devotee. Arjuna expresses the honesty and the purity of his love with respect, reverence and innocence. He feels that the Lord has possessed him at every level of his consciousness. He understands for the first time that his life is indeed meant to serve Lord. This reminds me of some words by the great mystic poet Rabindranath Tagore, "I seem to have loved you in numberless forms, numberless times, in life after life, in age after age forever".

Arjuna sings the glories of the Lord from the depth of his heart in transcendence. His words are pure expression of genuine love, when a person goes beyond the limitations of his personal individuality into the realm of mutual intimacy with the Divine. He comes to the realization that he is a co-worker with God in the great work of eliminating negativity and destroying the wicked people and vicious cycle. Establishment of morality and Dharma is a cooperative enterprise of God and man. He is awakened to the truth that behind the veil of entire activity, it is the will of God which prevails and keeps everything in motion. Every little bit of activity revolves around the will of the Divine—every change that takes place in life is an expression of the Lord's will.

Sri Kṛṣṇa tells Arjuna that the vision of the Supreme Lord comes as a blessing to the person who is totally devoted to the Lord, who lives in God and works through the guidance of the Lord. He says : *jnatum drastum ca tattvena pravestum ca parantapa.*—O' Arjuna only by sincere undivided devotion a person understands Me, perceives Me in essence and enters into My essentiality. This is what *Vedas* have declared—Being Becoming and Bliss.

Dhyana is of two types : (1) Saguna
dhyana—meditation on God with form and
attributes, and (2) Nirguna dhyana—meditation
on God without form and attributes.

Doing breath suspension and meditation on the
deity is saguna dhyana, and meditation on the
Supreme being without form is nirguna dhyana.
Nirguna dhyana leads to *samadhi*.

— Yogatattvopnishad 105

6

The Glory of Devotion

Bhagawad Geeta, Chapter 12
Bhaktiyoga

The dialogue opens with a question from Arjuna, he says, "O'Kṛṣṇa, some worship You with sincere undivided devotion and some others meditate on the unmanifest—which one of these two is the better knower of yoga?" This is the most common question asked by a person during his pursuit of spiritual journey. The anxiety to explore the relative worth of the two types of worshippers has been a perennial quest of many. Arjuna wants to know the comparative relevance of devotional services offered to the personal God and contemplation upon the unmanifest Divinity. As a student of Vedic tradition, Arjuna has been always taught that the Supreme Soul is attributeless, formless, omniscient and omnipresent; but after visualizing the God's cosmic form, his old concept has taken a new meaning. Although throughout the conversation, Sri Kṛṣṇa explained the worship of personal form of God but apparently Arjuna has missed the inner meaning of His statement. He is convinced that devotion to personal God is the best approach in spiritual journey but he still wants Sri Kṛṣṇa to confirm it.

Sri Kṛṣṇa tells Arjuna, *"mayyaevesya mano ye mam"*— means those who concentrate their mind on Me, live in unity with Me; are steadfast in their faith; worship Me with undivided devotion, are the knower of yoga. He also enlightens Arjuna about the devotion to the unmanifest and says that those who worship the imperishable, the indefinable, the unthinkable, the immovable, omniscient, and eternal with complete self-control, they also reach Me. As a matter of fact, in spiritual pursuit, as the worshipper makes progress in spirituality from less awareness to increased awareness, the 'One' being worshipped also changes, till he goes into the shrine within his own self. It is indeed difficult to draw a line between the worship of *saguna* and the meditation on *nirguna,* at which point one ends and the other starts.

In the process of worshipping *saguna* means God with form and name, we actually meditate on *nirguna*, the formless, who hides behind the *saguna*. By being devoted to either one, is indeed worshipping the both at the same time. It is after performing the worship of Lord with name and form for some time, when we learn to live in the consciousness of the Lord we understand the 'ideal' behind the 'idol'. The worship of God with name and form, spontaneously leads us to the worship of that which is at the heart of entire creation. For example, in some states of India, especially in Maharashtra and Bengal, there is a *visarjana* ceremony which forms the culmination of worship. During the *Navaratras* people worship various forms of gods and goddesses made of clay. After worship for nine days, all deities are taken in a procession to the river or to the nearby sea coast for *visarjana*. The word *visarjana* practically means immersion of idols, giving away the concept of forms and names. It is like rising above, from the worship of idol to the ideal, from less awareness to increased awareness.

In this connection, Swami Vivekananda has given a very good example. He tells that a man while going towards the sun takes a new photograph after every thousand miles and disregards the previous one till he reaches very close to the real sun! All pictures, although a little different from each other, are true. In fact, they are made to appear different by the changing conditions of time and space. Similarly, when the sincere devotee goes in Holy Communion with the Supreme-Self, he needs less and less help in the form of signs and symbols for concentration. He accelerates himself to a specific level of awareness where he feels the presence of God to be the essentiality of everything.

There is a story in our *Puranas* which explains it clearly. Once Lord Rama, the God-incarnate, asked his great devotee Hanuman, "O' son tell me what is your relationship with Me and how you meditate on Me. Sri Hanuman replied, "O' Rama, sometime I look upon You as '*Purna*', the undivided 'One', but at other moment I see your presence reflecting through everything and everybody and I look upon myself as a fragment of You. Yet another time, I meditate on You as my Divine Master and think of myself as Your humble servant. When, however, I am blessed with inner unity and the experiential knowledge of the Self then I feel that 'I am Thou' and 'Thou art I'— *Tattvamasi* ". It is a fact that in course of spiritual progress, the Supreme-Self reveals itself by itself to itself. The great scholar and educationist, Dr. Radhakrishnan, writes, "Once you realize that Reality is something to be felt, something to be experienced, you do not attach much importance to the method by which you attain it. They become subordinate and merely instrumental". People give different names to God in the process of their spiritual pursuit. The form of approach differs from one individual to another depending upon his own personal level of understanding. That's why Sri Ramakrishna used to say, it is just enough to have faith in God—many are the names of God and many are the methods through which one approaches the Divine. No one should argue on the issue that only my faith is correct and all others are wrong. The crescents, the crosses and symbols are only some visual aids for strengthening spiritual concepts.

The Absolute Truth is indeed beyond the reach of sensory perception. It is formless, nameless, and inexplicable. Either the person has to rise above finite boundaries, and experience the infinite, or to bring the infinite to the level of finite perception in some form. The ancient religious literature explains that the sages who wrote the Vedic hymns have described the God as Omnipresent, Omniscient and inexplicable. But later on the sages like *Vashist, Vyasa, Kashyap, Atri, Bharadwaj, Angirasa* and

Bhrigu believed in God both as *saguna and nirguna*—God with form and name, and God without form. These wise sages had deep experience of both *saguna* and *nirguna* and never had any arguments. *Yogatattvopanishad* gives a beautiful description, "Dhyana is of two types : *saguna dhyana,* meditation on God with form and attributes, and *nirguna dhyana,* meditation on God without form and attributes. Doing breath suspension and meditation on the deity is *saguna dhyana,* and meditation on the supreme being without form is *nirguna dhyana. Nirguna dhyana* leads to Samadhi". Sri Kṛṣṇa has mentioned earlier "*Ye yatha mam prapadyante tamstathai va bhajamy aham*". As people approach Me so do I seek them. The reason why Sri Kṛṣṇa expresses the concept of *saguna* and then immediately, the concept of *nirguna* because he knows that in the process of spiritual growth it is a natural progression to move from one concept to another.

In the process of meditation on the unmanifest, we move from the subtle to the gross, from the indwelling-Self to the cosmic-Self, while in the other approach of personal worship of God, we move from the gross to the subtle and from the subtle to the gross again with an experience of realizing the omniscience of the Lord in the universe. A true devotee of the Lord exhilarates in the personal experience of closeness with Divine and celebrates the joy of intimacy from moment to moment. For him the presence of God becomes experiential, real and enjoyable.

With reference to His explanation about the worship of God with form and shape and God without form and shape, Sri Kṛṣṇa expresses his concern for the devotees who meditate on the omniscient, inexplicable and unmanifest for the experiential knowledge of the self in yogic unity. By using the words, *"Klesoadhikataras tesam avyaktasakta-cetasam"*, He alerts mankind that the experience of yogic unity in meditation is very difficult as long as we hold our identification with the physical body. This attachment starts right after birth and becomes stronger as we grow older. Attachment with the body is *'dehabhimana'*, the feeling of 'I and Mine'. It comes as an obstacle in the process of communion with God, becomes a veil between the *Nara* and *Narayana*. This reminds me of some words from the poetry of a great Sufi poet Omar Khayyam, who says, "There was a door to which I found no key, there was a veil past which I could not see. Some talk awhile of me and Thee, There seemed—and then no more of Thee and me. It is Thee, in me who works behind, I lifted my veil to find, a lantern—amid the darkness, and cried—it is Me in thee blind."

In order to experience Holy Communion in yogic unity, the feeling of 'I and Mine' has to be replaced with 'Thou and Thine'. Sri Kṛṣṇa tells a wonderful method for this shift in awareness. He tells Arjuna, "Learn to live in the awareness of the Self and perform all the work with the consciousness of the Supreme-Self". It is subtle training of accepting the presence of Lord and also living in the consciousness of God at the same time. Swami Chinmayananda gives a very good example: "A dancer never forgets the rhythm of the drum to which she steps, a musician is ever conscious of the background hum. Thus living with awareness of the Divine, the mind operates directly under the guidance of the Supreme Divinity". Perfection in Yoga is definitely the perpetual absorption in the Lord. The Bliss of living a life in the consciousness of the Divine is indeed very rewarding, but it does not take place all at-once. There is a process. It is a step by step spiritual progress. The individual also has to learn to live in the presence of God every single minute of his life. It is the spontaneous love for the Divine, which brings transformation in the attitude of the individual. It is not the attitude of calculated services, it is the relationship of undivided love and devotion which brings transformation and initiates the individual into the spirit of selfless service.

With reference to the methods of concentration on the self, Sri Kṛṣṇa explains some methods that can be useful in training of yogic communion. He starts with *Abhyasayoga,* which means constant practice with repeated effort of living in the consciousness of Divine. It is to repeat the process of introducing a spiritual thought to the conscious and subconscious faculty of mind. Repeat the name of the Divine consciously and witness the process. Constant remembrance of the Lord purifies mind and creates the most intimate relationship with the Divine. Man or woman, literate or illiterate, ignorant or enlightened, rich or poor, everyone can use this method with equal benefit. As explained earlier, it may sound strange to some people, but it is the truth that progressive realization of the Divinity comes easily by the simple and natural method of remembering the Lord perpetually. Practice makes perfect. In the modern sustainable educated societies, sometimes it happens that the so-called intellectuals, and learned scholars, fail to accept the spiritual power of something so simple, as calling upon God with repetition of the holy mantra. With their egocentric explanations, they generally remain deprived of spiritual intimacy with the Supreme. Constant practice of remembering God keeps the individual aligned to the essence of life and makes yogic communion spontaneous and easy. Although in the initial stages it demands conscious efforts but gradually it just becomes second nature and consciousness of God is felt at all times. By placing the yoga of practice up-front in hierarchy, Sri Kṛṣṇa has presented a wonderful method of meditative unity for the people.

He makes it clear that true devotion and yogic communion becomes possible with faith, willingness and acceptance. When we accept to live in the consciousness of the Divine, we naturally dedicate all our work as a service to the Divine which liberates us from the bondage of karma—our every action becomes the yoga of action. There are people in every community who are constantly serving others. For them the opportunity to serve God becomes a blessing. For them selfless service to mankind becomes the worship of God.

Sri Kṛṣṇa tells Arjuna that just to accept the idea of God is not enough, let the idea pervade and permeate the individual. The person should learn to live a life which is completely aligned to the voice of the indwelling-self. *Uttama sahja avastha, Dwitya dhyana dharna* says Dr. Radhakrishnan that is, the state of perpetual connectedness with the indwelling supreme divinity comes first and then concentration in meditation. Live soaked in the nature of the Divine; do not have an instant of life separated from the Divine. Sri Aurobindo has called this *Sayujya Mukti*; it is all kinds of union at once. *Sahja avastha* means learning to live in a relaxed flow of awareness. It is being consciously aware of the inner peace and sensitive to the silent call of the Divine.

Explaining various methods for unity in yoga, Sri Kṛṣṇa concludes that knowledge is indeed better than that practice which is followed without proper insight. Meditation is of course superior to knowledge but renouncing attachment to the fruits of actions is even better; *tyaga chantir rantiram*—with renunciation peace follows quickly. He tells Arjuna that all spiritual austerities should be performed with proper insight and knowledge. As a matter of fact, the scriptural knowledge which is not used in the functioning of day-to-day activities remains mere information. It is of very little value. It is the meditative experience which reveals the inner knowledge of the Self and helps in proper understanding of scriptures. Meditation practice leads intellect into the subtle realms of increased awareness where the knowledge from books and teachers becomes subjective and experiential. It is indeed a fact that spontaneous inward assimilation of scriptural knowledge takes place only through contemplation and meditation. It allows the truth to be revealed naturally and effortlessly.

Meditation means to attend the thoughts with attention and intention. It is one of the greatest art of life in which we become introduced to our own self in all dimensions and can properly evaluate situations and circumstances of life as they arise. In the words of Swami Vishnu Devananda, "Meditation is the practice by which there is constant observation of the mind. It means focusing the mind on one point, calming the mind in order to perceive the Self. By stopping the waves of thoughts you come to understand your true nature and discover the wisdom and tranquillity that lie within". Meditation is not merely a religious practice. It is a necessity of life which ushers the individual into the realms of deep physical and mental relaxation bringing peace, harmony, inner contentment, success and fulfilment in everyday life. Daily meditation purifies the mind, body and emotions while providing the basis for more dynamic, productive and satisfying results of activities. It improves our general health, strengthens our immune system, helps us eliminate the stress from mind and body while increasing energy and vitality. It rejuvenates the body and promotes reversal of aging. It improves memory, intellectual abilities, creativity and comprehension.

Daily meditation and yoga practice promotes orderly thinking with clarity of thoughts and brings spontaneous psychological changes at various levels of consciousness. Yoga meditation has been glorified in the ancient scriptures of India. It is one of the highest forms of discipline which comes with the practice of living in constant awareness of the Self.

The goal in meditation is to observe the activities of mind and guide the mind and body into inner peace and silence. Although each person has the ability to meditate naturally, but in general people find it very difficult to concentrate and meditate. For them, meditation period goes in vain, with the mind struggling to settle in the serenity of the Self. In general the meditator has to struggle with the internal gossip, which comes from our relationship with other people and from the day-to-day activities of life. Out of the total half hour of meditation period they can really meditate for only one or two minutes, the rest of the time they are with their co-workers, friends or in argument with their friends and relatives. Our entire lifestyle, I mean the way we live and handle our day-to-day problems, actually determines the content of meditation. Sri Kṛṣṇa the knower of human emotional make-up understands this problem. That is why in the description of methods for *yogic* unity in meditation He declares that renouncing attachment to the fruits of actions is the key for perfection in *yogic* unity with the Self; because it eliminates the sources of unrest and brings about dynamic quietude which is the foundation of meditative life. Gospel of selfless action definitely leads to the subordination of all other methods used by the aspirant in spiritual journey. Detachment promotes inner silence and helps in concentration guiding the mind into profound contemplation which brings peace quickly. *Tyaga chantra rantram.* In reference to this concept of success in meditation with attitude of detachment and desireless action the great educationist Wayne Dyer says, "I find God by giving myself time every day—through prayer, or meditation, or whatever you want to call it—to go into another level of consciousness. I close my eyes and breathe. I centre myself and empty my mind and begin to feel the love that is there when I quiet down enough to feel. As I do this I transcend time and space, and I am in the very presence of God. This, to me, is a direct daily experience of God, and it puts me into a state of harmony and bliss that transcends anything I have ever known". For inner peace and harmony he adds "the highest spiritual act in life is to see yourself in everyone else and everyone else in you, to surrender yourself and see everyone's joy and suffering as your own, to detach yourself from your ego-need to be attached to the fruits of your labour, and to simply see every one else in the world as part of you. You renounce all worldly attachments to everything and enjoy what God gives you. You just constantly flow through your life without getting attached to the results. The irony is that the less attached you are, the more you get. The more you keep circulating, the more keeps coming back to you. It is a flowing system".

The attitude of performing actions without attachment is very difficult. It does not happen all at once. It doesn't take place just by talking about it. There is a subtle training of perpetually living in the consciousness of God with love and devotion and performing all duties as a service to God and fellow beings. The process involves the spirit of unconditional love and devotion to God. When life becomes totally devoted to the Supreme Lord the consecration of all works to the Lord becomes a way of life. As consciousness of the presence of Divine blossoms, the entire lifestyle becomes a constant remembrance of the Divine. When the aspirant advances in unification with the Divine, the spirit of renunciation to the fruits of actions takes place quite effortlessly and spontaneously. The inner unity, peace and security, helps the individual to rise above the futility of worldly name, fame and the desire of recognition. As a matter of fact, the Gospel of selfless action works as a remarkable tool in any method of worship whichever the person chooses for God-realization. Almost all other methods revolve around it and draw their completeness from it. Renunciation of the fruits of all actions is indeed the touchstone of success in spiritual life. I like these words of Lao Tzu, 'Do your work and step back, the only path to serenity".

After giving a short description of what is devotion and how we can become devoted to the Lord, Sri Kṛṣṇa gives a detailed description about the hallmarks of a genuine devotee. These are the characteristic features of a man of sincere devotion and guidelines for spiritual progress. He starts from the word *adveshta* which literally means no jealousy. A true devotee of the Lord who is perpetually aligned with the essential nature of the Higher-Self, is very peaceful, secure, contented, and simply likes himself the way he is. He never compares and competes with anybody. In this reference I like what Ralph Emerson says, "There is a time in every man's education when he arrives at the conviction that envy is ignorance; that imitation is suicide; that he must take himself for better for worse as his portion; that though the wide universe is full of good, no kernel of nourishing corn can come to him but through his toil bestowed on that plot of ground which is given to him to till. The power which resides in him is new in nature, and none but he knows what that is, which he can do, nor does he know until he has tried".

A person of unswerving devotion is also very generous, kind, caring and compassionate. It is indeed a fact that anybody, who is settled in unity with God, naturally becomes settled in unity with the whole universe. He looks upon the entire creation as a living organism united within the essentiality of the Supreme Lord. He is very friendly, loving, caring and sympathetic. Anybody who is aligned with *prajña*, which is a specific level of increased awareness; his conscious unity with *prajña* reflects itself in *karuna*, which is love, compassion and generosity towards his fellow beings. The sympathetic attitude of sharing is the expressive aspect of spiritual intimacy, one holds with his own inner-self. The enlightened devotee of the Lord develops cosmic unity and touches the heart of entire creation with love and kindness.

The other characteristics of a true devotee is *sama-duhkha-sukhah kshami* means balanced in pleasure and pain and also forgiving. A true devotee of the Lord who is grounded in the consciousness of the Divine, definitely becomes very strong both psychologically and physically. Each new day brings something new to the life of an individual who lives in unity with God. He knows how to live in the tissue of the present moment and make the best use of everything as it comes along. This reminds me of some beautiful lines by a Chinese poet, "thousands of beautiful flowers in spring, cool breeze in summer, moon in autumn, and snow in winter—if your mind is not clouded by unnecessary things this is the most enjoyable moment of your life". It is indeed a fact that one who feels secure within, can live in perfect peace, amid the ups and downs of life. Sri Krṣṇa has used the word *santustah* for contentment. There is no treasure equal to contentment in this world. The person who lives in unity with the pure luminous nature of the Supreme-Self, becomes very appreciative and thankful. A thankful heart is indeed a contented heart. I like these words from *Gitanjali* by Tagore, "Day by day thou art making me worthy of the simple, great gifts that thou gavest to me unasked—this sky and the light, this body and the life". Contentment is indeed a blessing of the Divine. Contentment makes life richer, broader, larger and lovable. It promotes inner wisdom, faith, courage and longevity. Anyone who is truly contented will not develop tensions, anxieties, insecurities, fears and worries. Contentment is promoted from inner peace, security and tranquillity. There is a famous saying "a contented person is not necessarily the one who has the best of everything; he just makes the best of whatever he has". Contentment can be recognized as inner enlightenment. Lao Tzu says : "when you are content to be simply yourself and don't compare or compete, everybody will respect. Chase after money and security and your heart will never unclench. Care about people's approval and you will be their prisoner. If you realize that you have enough, you are truly rich".

Another important thing is that a person who lives in peace and harmony with the Self, respects law and order in society and helps others to live in harmony with each other. As a matter of fact when the mind and intellect are anchored to the Divine, a person naturally works through the guidance of the Divine. His inclination towards a virtuous, spiritual and ethical living comes without much effort and for him obedience to moral law comes instinctively. He does not have to wrestle to be ethical and spiritual, it happens spontaneously. Anybody who is settled in the tranquillity of the Self, lives a very peaceful and balanced life. All his work confirms to the maintenance of spiritual law of the Divine. A serene joy radiates from his work, equanimity and compassion for humanity becomes second nature for him. No one ever gets agitated by his words and deeds; also he himself is not agitated by others. His inner peace and integrity are rooted to the consciousness of his faith and in the experiential knowledge of its realization.

Sri Kṛṣṇa glorifies the greatness of yogic unity in devotion and makes it clear to Arjuna that a sincere devotee of the Lord is very skilful and meticulous. Excellence in work is a state of mind which comes from self-reliance, self-respect and faith in our own selves; self confidence comes from our faith in God and with our perpetual alignment to the source of life. Our experience of unity with the Supreme-Soul gives us confidence, inner satisfaction, creativity and perfection in each and every one of our activity. Those who don't enjoy their work have definitely lost their conscious alignment with God in them. The inner emptiness results into lack of self-respect, self-reliance, self-confidence, enthusiasm and creativity in work. They become careless and sluggish and stop taking pride in their work. The quality of their work goes down. Excellence in the performance of work is a clear reflection of the inner unity to the source of life. A person in unity becomes devoted to his work and performs his duties with great enjoyment. He takes pride in his work and his work becomes very creative, enjoyable and rewarding. He knows how to explore his unique abilities and put them to best use. What generally people call intelligence, good luck or destiny, in fact, it is the depth of communion one holds with one's own inner-self.

With reference to emotional maturity, Sri Kṛṣṇa tells Arjuna that a man who is grounded in unity with the Self, is mature, impartial and determined. He makes quick, wise and very mature decisions. Maturity is increased awareness and heightened intuition. Intuition, as the word explains, is education from within which is revealed from the source of life by our own personal effort. It is the grace of the Divine which becomes revealed in the form of inner knowledge and maturity. In general people believe that maturity comes with age, that is true to some extent; but it is also true that there is a great majority of people who do not mature with age. Lack of maturity reflects lack of self-confidence, and lack of self-confidence reflects lack of faith in one's own self. An overall maturity in life is in direct proportion to the alignment with the Supreme-Self.

Sri Kṛṣṇa tells Arjuna that anybody who is firmly settled in the transcendental wisdom of the Self, becomes very enlightened; his emotional life is guided by the

awareness of the Supreme and his adjustment to the
circumstances becomes quite spontaneous and natural. A
true devotee of God understands all intrigues of life and
also perfectly knows that he himself is the cause of every
situation as it occurs. He does not blame others for his
failures and misfortunes. He neither complains nor worries
over the inevitable that lies hidden in distant future. He
rises above the trivial changes of day-to-day life. His
experiential knowledge of the Higher-Self liberates him
from all sorts of pains and fears.

In general, love for one person and hatred for the
other comes up when we calculate the situation from our
limited point of view. To like or dislike someone is a
totally personal conditioned behaviour which can be
eliminated by living in the awareness of the Higher-self. A
person who lives in the awareness of the indwelling pure
luminous Self, he lives in alignment with the purity of the
self in others. He becomes kind, friendly, and
compassionate; radiates unusual spiritual wisdom which
brings peace and solace to the people around him.

Sri Krṣṇa tells Arjuna that another important quality
which characterizes the man in unity with the Supreme-
spirit is that he maintains his balance of mind in honour
and dishonour. He is always calm and peaceful enjoying

the Elysian Bliss of Divine Communion. As a matter of fact human mind evaluates and equates a situation as honourable or dishonourable in direct proportion to the self-created gauge of conditioned thinking. A simple remark about some one's car or house can be considered as an appreciation and also a cynical criticism at the same time. A person, who is aligned with the source of life, remains emotionally integrated and he is not disturbed at the puny remarks made by other people. Fitzgerald explains this in beautiful words, "the true test of a first rate mind is the ability to hold two contradictory ideas at the same time". Alignment with the indwelling-Self dissolves all boundaries of egocentric-self and promotes the joy of living in eternity. There is an incident from the life story of a saint, who lived in a small cottage outside the town. One day someone stole his cooking pots, pans and other belongings. He went to the nearby police station to report the theft and get some help. The police clerk was very rude to him and also wanted some bribe for lodging the complaint. The holy man did not have any money and refused to pay. The police clerk did not treat the holy man with respect and ordered him to leave. After a few months, the clerk's son became very ill. Despite all treatment when the child's health was deteriorating fast some one suggested him to approach the holy saint who lived outside the town. The clerk decided to visit the saint. As he entered the cottage, he was shocked to see that the holy saint was the same person who had come earlier to the police station for some help. He felt ashamed of himself and begged for forgiveness. On the other hand, the holy man had forgotten all about it. As a matter of fact, he himself came forward to bless his son for speedy recovery. The enlightened saints who are always grounded in the consciousness of the Self, are usually very forgiving. Kindness and generosity of the Lord reflects through their words and deeds. Anybody who feels secure within his own self, he lives in peace and harmony with others. An illumined, spiritualized individual who is perennially settled in ecstasy of transcendental-Self is always caring, loving and forgiving. On the other hand, people who cannot forgive others are insecure and lack the strength of forgiving which comes from the bonding with the Higher-Self. A forgiving soul is indeed a blessed and liberated soul, who enjoys constant sweet, melodious communion with the Supreme and radiates Divine presence by his words and deeds. In this reference Rabindranath Tagore says : "I sat alone in the corner of my house, thinking it too small for any stranger to come, but now with thy grace when the door is flung open, I feel there is room for the entire world". Forgiveness is a great gift of God. To forgive is to feel free like a cloud wandering in the open sky.

Sri Kṛṣṇa tells Arjuna that a sincere devotee of the Lord understands that the life flows between two poles—pleasure and pain, and loss and gain. He accepts life as it comes along. He believes in the truth that there is a purpose behind each and every situation whether it is favourable or unfavourable. I like these words of Viktor E. Frankl a great German psychologist, "if there is a meaning in life at all, then there must be a meaning in suffering". He further says, "no one should think that these considerations are unworldly and too far removed from real life. It is true that only a few people are capable of reaching such high moral standards". This strength of the enlightened devotee is called the inner awakening which comes with the grace of the Divine. Living in the remembrance of the Supreme Lord, brings the experience of living in eternity, which is far above the changing phases of the material world. When attitude towards life becomes enlightened it brings changes in the entire outlook of a person. He gives a totally new meaning to the ups and downs of life. The inner peace and tranquillity of mind helps him to remain undisturbed in all situations and under all circumstances. Maharishi Mahesh

Yogi supports this concept in these words, "Just as a millionaire who has great wealth remains unaffected by the rise and fall of the market, so the mind which has gained the state of bliss-consciousness through Transcendental Meditation remains naturally contented on coming out from the transcendental state to the field of activity. This contentment, being grounded in the very nature of the mind, does not allow the mind to waver and be affected in pleasure or pain; nor allow it to become affected by attachment or fear in the world. This natural equanimity of the mind, even while it is actively engaged, is the state of steady intellect".

Sri Kṛṣṇa has used the word *Mauni* once again for the sincere devotee who knows how to observe silence. It is not only the silence of speech; it also refers to the quietness of mind. *Mauna* is an alignment with the silence of the Self from where we receive guidance. About silence, I like these words of Gandhiji, "Experience has taught me that silence is a part of spiritual discipline. Silence is both a physical and a spiritual necessity. The time when I could hold best communion with God, has been indeed during the time of silence *(mauna vrata)*". Mauna *vrata* heightens awareness and makes one receptive to the inner knowledge of the Self. *Mauni* is the one who observes silence; it stands for the illumined sage who has a total control over his speech and mind.

The next hallmark of an enlightened devotee is inner integrity and determination. A true devotee of the Lord is very determined, confident and sure of his each and every activity; precept and practice go together for him. For example, all the great teachers of the world like Socrates, Plato, the Buddha, Shankaracharya, Jesus Christ and Mahatma Gandhi have been believers in their own thoughts. Gandhiji believed in himself and was always sure that every word, which he spoke, came from the honesty of his heart. He always believed that he worked in copartnership with God; and whatever has been true for him must be true for others as well. He was always positive, firm and determined about his ideas because he felt that God has been working through him. In one of his speeches during the Dandi March he said, "I have faith in the righteousness of our cause and the purity of our weapons. Where the means are clean there God undoubtedly is present with His blessings and where the two combine there defeat is impossibility". A man of steadfastness becomes very familiar with the power of providence and knows how to express divine ideas through his words and deeds. His life is tuned to the Divine symphony and his words are always clear and influential. He is constantly aware of his goals and moves ahead with full confidence. Steadfastness, conformity and self-reliance are great virtues and a great blessing of the Divine.

Sri Kṛṣṇa concludes that the thirty-nine hallmarks of a true devotee are indeed the codes of primordial *Dharma*. It should be the endeavour of every one to live a life which is grounded in the consciousness of the indwelling Supreme-Self and primordial *Dharma*. Living a life in conformity to the voice of the Supreme-Self is indeed living by the code of *Dharma*. Performing all duties with the guidance of the Supreme-Self is the *Dharma* of mankind.

There are two selves lodged in the secret chambers of the heart involved in world of actions. The knowers of *Brahman*, speak of them as shade and light.

— *Kathopnishad 1.3.1*

7

The Body is a Field
&
The Masks of the Conditioned-Self

Bhagawad Geeta, Chapter 13 & 14
Ksetra-Ksetrajna-Vibhaga-Yoga & Guna-Triya-Vibhagayoga

The Body is a Field :
The dialogue opens with the words of Sri Kṛṣṇa : *Idam sariram Kaunteya kshetram ity abhidhiyate*-O' Arjuna, this body is a field. A modern physicist describes the field as an abstraction which expresses the forces of nature. According to a physicist everything in the universe is expressed through a field. There are many fields of forces such as the gravitational field, the electromagnetic field and the quantum field. Any type of force is manifested through a field only. So we can describe the field as an abstraction which takes any form and shape in respect of the cause, effect and time.

The word field which is used by a physicist to describe the most well-known forces of nature has also been used by Sri Kṛṣṇa in relation to the forces that express through the bodies of all beings. The physical body is a field—a manifestation of the forces of mind, intellect and ego. When Einstein was trying to describe the unified field from where all other fields draw their power, he wrote, "My religion is a humble admiration of that who reveals Himself in the slightest detail we are able to perceive with our frail and feeble mind". While using the word field for the body, Sri Kṛṣṇa tells Arjuna about the condition in nature which has the potential of producing a force which is called the field.

As we see, people usually feel surprised over the phenomenon of life—as from where it comes and where it goes? What is destiny? Why there is so much disparity among human beings in relation to looks, intelligence, capabilities and potentialities? Although born from the same parents, why all brothers and sisters are so different from one another. Sri Kṛṣṇa answers to all these questions. He tells Arjuna that physical, psychological and causal bodies constitute the totality of the field. The physical body is a field of expression of the invisible forces of the subtle body. The subtle body is a field of thoughts, memories, latencies and *samskaras*, that find their expression into the field of physical body. The thoughts and memories become *samskaras* and the *samskaras* give shape to *karmas* and the *karmas* are expressed as destiny. The physical body is only an expression of some thoughts and memories, enclosed in mind.

Subtle body is a field of information. Each person is different because of his own personal data which he records and stores in the field of information. Every single thought that goes through the mind, is duly recorded and saved in the field of information and later expressed in action. The recorded data in mind give shape to all the activities of daily life. Every expression in physical body has its roots in the data of the subtle body which is a field of memories, and *samskaras*. If we closely observe the entire span of life till date, we can realize that the entire life is only a bundle of memories. Every single moment of life becomes a memory. Last year, last week, yesterday and till last few hours of even today, every moment has become some kind of memory and *samskara*. All the years of great joy, the most cherished moments of life, the most difficult suffering, every minute has become a memory which has been duly recorded and saved in the field of subtle body—the memory bank.

Sri Kṛṣṇa tells Arjuna, that the entire life is a vast field of actions and also revolves around the wheel of thoughts, memories and *samskaras*. Just as a seed yields the corresponding type of crop the memories saved in the field of information take shape into actions and yield their fruits in due course of time. No one can escape the law of *karmas*. People reward and punish themselves because of their own *karmas*. It is the law of cause and effect which gives momentum to the wheel of creation.

There is a true incident that relates this truth. Once there lived a rich man who had two sons. After his death his entire estate was equally given to both the sons. After a few years the younger brother died leaving his young widow. One evening the elder brother went to her house and killed his sister-in-law. At night he wrapped the body and dumped it in a pool nearby. Nobody suspected anything and naturally he escaped punishment. Later on, he decided to leave the village for sometime and went to another place. There he started his own business. One day while he was driving back home, he noticed a young lady crying for help on the road side. He parked his car and rushed to help her. As he approached and gave her some water to drink, she opened her eyes for a few minutes but died instantly. Some people gathered around the dead body and called the police. After going through all investigations the police arrested the young man. After many trials the law declared death penalty for him. The day when authorities were going to put him in electric chair he was asked for the last wish. He cried and said I surely want to tell the entire world that it is the law of cause and effect which prevails at the heart of entire creation. Nobody can ever escape the law of *karma*. No matter where one goes, the guilt and crime goes with the person and punishment comes in due time. He further added, believe me, I have not killed this woman but this punishment indeed is justified because I had killed another woman, a few years ago and had escaped punishment at that time. The law of karma is indeed very powerful. The ultimate truth is, 'as we sow so we reap'. Every one is bound by the cycle of cause and effect.

Earlier in the dialogue Sri Kṛṣṇa has explained to Arjuna about the immortality of the soul, here He repeats the same truth in a different way. He says—those who know the reality of this body as a field and the one who controls this body as the knower of the field, he is called a man of wisdom. He further explains to Arjuna, about the mysteries of various fields, the interconnection of these fields and how each one is sustained by the knower of the field. The concept of relativity declares for sure, that one should aim at looking into the truth for himself and not to accept everything based upon the inherited habits of perceptual thinking about the world. Sri Kṛṣṇa wants Arjuna to pursue the validity of the knower of the field and gets introduced with that. He wants Arjuna to be awakened from the systematic self-deceptive explanations of conditioned-self and engage into the subtlest adventure of perceiving the one beyond the masks of eternity. The *Para Brahman* is beyond and above the boundaries of mind, body and ego.

Sri Kṛṣṇa explains to Arjuna how life force manifests through everything that can be seen, touched, tasted and experienced through the senses. The knower of the field is indeed the energizer, who experiences all sense-objects, but still remains detached and aloof as a silent witness. Super power can be experienced by everyone through the functions of the sensory organs, and still transcends everything. The world is created, maintained and sustained by that power still that knower acts only as a witness. Sri Kṛṣṇa draws Arjuna's attention to the knower of the field, who is perceived being manifested in creation. Whatever comes into existence, living or non-living, emanates from the union of the field and the knower of the field. Although the field of matter is insentient but when the spirit plays through the field, it energizes the same. On the surface it may appear that the Supreme Spirit has become the field but in essence it maintains its essential aloofness.

The field and the knower of the field both exist in a mystical union. Einstein, the well-known scientist, says :

"the observer enters into every observation. All the experiences of everything in creation are coupled with experiencing the Self because both are indeed inseparably fused in each and every perception". For example, when the person sits in meditation, the Self watches the person trying to meditate. It observes all efforts, all struggles, failures and successes. Even in transcendental meditation the Self observes each and every movement of the person while entering into trance. A deep insight makes it clear that the Self transcends all experiences and also the flow of time in which all activities take place. The change can be perceived only by the one who is changeless, the mutation can be perceived only by the one who is immutable.

When we are introduced to our essential nature as the knower of the field we live as a spectator, as a witness and give our self a chance for self-analysis and self-improvement. We also experience the essential truth that 'I am separate from the body and I am the knower of the body', and that is when our real education begins. Self-realization is to be able to realize the Self as the witness of all activities. So it is essential to have a clear understanding of the distinction between the thought and the one who is aware of that thought. Rishis—the knower of this truth—have declared gloriously, *"Na mai deha, Na mai deha ke Dharma, na mai prana na indriyas karma, na mai mana budhi chitha ahankara, gunatita mai ina sai nayara"*. It means I am neither this body nor the functions of this body. I am neither the *prana*—means the vital breath nor the functions of the senses—I am neither mind, nor intellect, ego or the masks of nature. I am above cause, space, time and the witness of all.

While describing glories of the knower of the field Sri Kṛṣṇa says "light of all lights", Supreme-Self is beyond darkness. God is knowledge, the object of knowledge and also the goal of all knowledge. Although present everywhere, He can be intimated as seated at the shrine of heart. The same description occurs in dialogue between *Rishi Uddalaka* and his son *Svetaketu* in *Chhandogyopanisad* : "Do you know, by knowing which everything else is known"? Knowing God and knowing a friend or a son or daughter may appear different on surface but all of them are known only through the study of the Self. Self-realization which transcends the conditioned experiences gradually becomes spiritual endeavour. It is only with the experiential knowledge of the Lord within that makes all other experiences of life meaningful; and all staggering notions of the absolute truth intelligible and vividly clear.

Sri Kṛṣṇa declares the heart to be the dwelling place

of the Supreme-Self in body. *Vedas* and *Upanisads* have also indicated that the Supreme-soul is seated in everyone's heart. In ancient scriptures of India as well as in other religious traditions of the world, concentration on the heart centre has been highly emphasized. The heart centre is also known as the *anahat chakra* in yogic terminology. It is from the *anahat chakra*, that the primordial sound of *Aum* can be heard very clearly and vividly. In meditation session, as the individual concentrates deeply into the silent realms of the heart, the sound of *Aum* becomes very clear and alluring. It is in meditation on the sound of *Aum*, the experience of the presence of the Supreme soul at the shrine of heart becomes real and exhilarating. When the awareness gets settled into the sound of the eternal *nada*, the yogic experience of alignment with the indwelling soul becomes rich and rewarding. There is a similar type of description given by Jesus Christ also, "discover the Lord in your heart and then in the heart of thy neighbour". It is at the heart centre, the act of purification starts and the spirit of surrender takes place. It is at the heart centre where man is remade. It is at the heart centre where love for God is awakened and the presence of the Divine is personally experienced and we become sensitive to the needs of other people. Other people also become aware to the light at our shrine and we become a channel of sharing divine love with others. The experience of unity at the heart centre is the most cherished accomplishment in the spiritual journey.

After giving a long description of the field and the knower of the field, Sri Kṛṣṇa tells Arjuna that the presence of the Lord in body can be felt as playing various roles at different levels of consciousness, such as observer, controller, spectator and Lord of the entire creation. The expression *upadrasta* literally means the silent witness. When the individual soul simply observes all the thoughts going in and out of the mind, and beholds all the actions in body; the soul acts as a witness and is called *upadrasta*. For example, a person takes the role of an on-looker of his own mind and body when he relates subtle events of his dream, where the thoughts turn magically into things and forms. The power that gives validity to both dreaming and waking experience is one and the same silent on-looker. It is the same awareness (consciousness) which functions in both aspects. The silent on-looker describes even the dreamless sleep when the physical body and the subtle body both are at rest. Even in deep sleep there is someone who is witnessing the state of complete rest and perfect unity with the Higher-self. Who is that witness? This is indeed the silent indweller who resides in the hearts of all.

The other role is that of *anumanta* means the counsellor

who guides in all respects. The indwelling-self observes every single wisp of thought that flashes through the mind and acts as a guide to the individual in deciding what is right and what is wrong. He helps in making the right choices at the right time. The inner consciousness is called *bharta* who nurtures, sustains, and protects the body. When the individual-soul in the body simply observes the incoming desire, he is called the observer but when the embodied-soul becomes a participant in the fulfilment of that desire, the individual soul is called the enjoyer—the *bhokta* or the one who experiences. At that level of consciousness the individual soul *(jivatma)* becomes the enjoyer of pleasure and pain, loss and gain, honour and ignominy. As a controller of various functions in the body, the soul is also called *Mahesvarah*. The word *Mahesvarah* is self explanatory. *Maha* means the great and *Iswara* means the Lord. The indwelling-Self acts as the master of mind, intellect, ego, senses and all other organs that work for the maintenance of the body. When the soul goes into unity with the Supreme-Soul, *jivatma* is called *Paramatma*. It is the conscious unification of *jivatma* with the *Paramatma*. The *Paramatma* and the *atma* are both the same super power that controls everything and forms the essence of all life. Sri Kṛṣṇa emphasizes that with proper knowledge of the Supreme Spirit and the primordial nature one attains the discriminating ability which helps him to separate the unreal from the real, the conditioned from the unconditioned, and mortal from the immortal. He performs his duties in the light of the knowledge of the Self and in perfect communion with God. He lives his life as a witness and as an on-looker of his own mind and body. The individual who understands and perceives the Supreme-Soul and the manifested primordial nature separately, knower of the field and the field, definitely learns to live in the world with heart anchored to the knower of the field.

With reference to realization of the Self, as knower of the field Sri Kṛṣṇa explains different paths for God-realization and self-realization. He tells Arjuna that some people perceive the Self, by the Self, within the Self, through meditation, others by the Yoga of knowledge and yet some others by the Yoga of action. Also there are people who become devoted to the Lord by listening from others. They too attain the Supreme goal just by being devoted to whatever they hear from others. Meditation as discussed earlier is introspective contemplation, in which we try to observe and control the contents and the direction of our thoughts which leads towards inner silence and realization of the self. It helps us step by step to re-establish mastery over our lives beginning with an introduction to ourselves. In the words of Swami Vishnu Devananda, "with the continued practice of meditation you discover a greater sense of purpose and strength of will and your thinking becomes clearer and more concentrated affecting all you do".

There are no secrets or mysteries about learning meditation. It is a natural process of restoring inner peace and quietude which facilitates self-illumination. The guidelines for relaxed meditation followed by the yogins, saints, advanced meditators, and family men do vary to some extent but in general people have used the same steps since time immemorial. First of all, it is important to meditate once or twice a day on a regular schedule, using the same place and time each day. Early morning is the ideal time for meditation because it blends with nature's daily cycle of awakening to new life, as well as preparing ourselves peacefully for our own daily activities. Quietness across the horizon is very conducive to the natural rhythms of mind and body which makes meditation practice quite enjoyable and productive. The other auspicious time is *sandhya*—the sunset when the air is charged with spiritual energy and mind becomes receptive to the silent call of the divine. Evening time when we are relatively free from daily routine work, we must schedule an hour or so for relaxed moments of inner peace and unity in transcendence. Sit upright on a chair or in crossed legged posture, facing

east or north for enlightenment and stability. It also helps
in alignment with the earth's magnetic field. Regulate the
breathing pattern; inhaling and exhaling for about three to
five minutes instructing the mind to attend to breath. Pray
in a few words with concentration at the heart chakra and
move upward towards the *ajna chakra,* the space between
the two eyebrows. Gradually the internal chattering stops,
the mind calms down and starts enjoying the silence of the
Self. It is for sure a fact, that with regular practice the
grace of the Supreme-soul is revealed in the daily
meditation session and we are guided into the yogic unity.

Meditation is not just a religious practice. It is certainly
a necessity of life which helps the individual to organize
thoughts and actually determine what is important for his
well being. It is for sure a fact that helpful ideas
spontaneously come to the surface of awareness in
meditation, those intuitively guide us to make right choices
and perform right actions. With regular practice of
meditation our illusionary concepts begin to dissolve
gradually, we enter into the realm of pure consciousness
and tuned to the eternal status of Absolute Bliss. It helps
the person live in perfect harmony with his own self and
with others. Sri Kṛṣṇa tells Arjuna that some people seek
unity with the self by the yoga of action. A Karmayogi
perpetually lives in God and performs all his work with

the consciousness of God. He also knows how to go into silence of the Self whenever he wants. By using the word "*sruti-parayanah*", Sri Krsna makes it clear that longing for the yogic communion which is initiated from the purity of heart is indeed very powerful. It definitely brings transformation, self-realization and God-realization in due time. An honest attitude in prayer is the very essence of success to the goal of realization.

There are people who are not familiar with the techniques of meditation and they do not understand much about philosophies of the ancient scriptures but just by learning and listening from the saints and holy sages with faith and devotion, they attain God-realization and become eligible for liberation. Sri Krsna has mentioned earlier in the dialogue—*anukampayartham*—out of my compassion, I enlighten them about their *atmabhavastha*—true nature of the Self. Each and every person is an eligible candidate for the experience of communion and union with God. Everyone has inherent ability and capacity for inner awakening and enlightenment. The only thing which helps in spiritual growth is faith, willingness, genuine devotion and purity of heart. Sri Krsna assures that any one who goes in unity with the Self and understands the distinction between the body and the Master of the body becomes liberated in due course of time.

The knowledge of the Supreme-Self liberates the person from the intrigues of his conditioned behaviour. It is through experiential knowledge of the Supreme-Self that a person can attain liberation from the Xeroxed behaviour of his conditioned habits. It is a shift in understanding. It is a shift from bondage to freedom.

The Masks of the Conditioned-Self :

With reference to the masks of the conditioned Self, Sri Kṛṣṇa says *"Param bhuyah pravaksyami jñananam jñanam uttamam"*. O'Arjuna I must tell you more in detail about the Divine knowledge and wisdom. The transcendental knowledge of the Supreme-Self is within access of every human being. It is not something to be acquired from somebody else, it actually needs to be revealed to us from our own inner-Self. This knowledge of the Supreme-Self becomes alien to us because of our own negligence and ignorance. Introduction to the knowledge of the Self is the progressive realization from the conscious state of mind to the superconsciousness; from the conditioned finite awareness to infinite awareness. It is only when a person transcends the limitations of his physical body and the masks of the conditioned-self that he can comprehend the essentiality of his pure unconditioned nature and bliss of the Supreme Divinity.

Sri Kṛṣṇa enlightens Arjuna about the mystical union of spirit and matter and explains that every single expression of life in the universe is the Supreme Spirit manifesting through matter. He declares *Prakriti* (primordial nature) to be *the Mahat Brahma. Brahma* means expanding immeasurably. *Hiranyagarbha,* the cosmic womb of all beings, is the other name of *Brahma.* The individual subtle body, the field of information is the mind, intellect and ego. It is also called the causal body which is responsible for the creation of the gross body. The mind, intellect and ego are the channels through which every little sensation is perceived, received, processed, assimilated, metabolized and manifested through thoughts, words and deeds. The combination of all the subtle bodies in creation is the *hiranyagarbha,* or the *Mahat Brahma.* The primordial nature is the womb which becomes impregnated by the Lord of the universe. Mother Nature is the womb in which the Divine consciousness is seated as the seed-giving Father. It is the potency of the Divine which energizes the inert nature and makes it grow and manifest itself as the most spectacular creation. It is indeed the potency of the Supreme spirit which is being visually expressed in each and everything of the universe. The Lord himself is the Father of the universe who vitalizes and energizes the primordial nature, which in turn orchestrates the entire play in the universe. The multitude of beings comes into existence from the union of matter and the Supreme Spirit. One Supreme power becomes manifest through innumerable forms and shapes within various grades of potentialities bound by their own latencies. Matter is indeed the cosmic mother of the entire spectacular universe and *Iswara* is the cosmic father.

Everyone in the world is born from the union of Mother Nature and the Lord Himself as the Father. Just as a child inherits from both the parents, likewise we are born with the pure nature of the Supreme-Self, the conditioned nature of *panch mahabootas*—inherited from parents, and our own memories of previous births. When the soul takes up the human body, it becomes very attached to the body and wants to enjoy everything in the world. But being a fragment of the Divine, the conditioned spirit definitely feels comforted in the unity with the Supreme Spirit. In human body the individual-soul (*jivatma*) becomes confused because of various masks of conditioned behaviour and that is why sometime in the midst of all kinds of worldly enjoyments, a person feels lonely, and seeks his forgotten relationship. Being a fragment of the Supreme Lord an individual can rise to the height of a genius, but if he ignores the inner unity and the voice of the Supreme-Self, he can fall into the ditches of degradation. Every embodied-soul is potentially divine. The goal of human life is to experience closeness of the Divine and to live a life which is consciously aligned to the Supreme-soul. Any misalignment from the indwelling-Self results into conscious separation from the source of life and slavery to Xeroxed behaviour dictated by the conditioned-self.

Sri Kṛṣṇa tells Arjuna about the masks of the conditioned self. He talks about the instinctive nature of man. The thinking faculty of every person does express the qualities of Mother Nature, such as, *sattvic, rajasic and tamasic* (purity, passion and dark-inertia). All thoughts and activities of life are guided and processed by the three *gunas*. He tells Arjuna that it is very important to understand these qualities of matter, and the way we become conditioned by them. *Sattva* is pure light, illumination and enlightenment. It is generally represented by white colour. A *sattvic* person, is always in unity with the purity of Divine. He thinks clearly and can differentiate between right and wrong. For example, he knows the kind of food he should eat which is healthy for the body; and the type of books he should read and the kind of friends he should associate with. The study of spiritual literature, ethical behaviour, interest in learning, responsible performance of duties, constructive thinking, harmonious wholesome living are the characteristic of a *sattvic* person—a man of purity.

A *sattvic* person enjoys working for the welfare of mankind, such as providing free medical services for the poor; free supply of food, clothing and books etc. He always lives in the awareness of the Self and works in perfect harmony with others. He is very organized and his goals are very clear to him. He is always very positive, cheerful and at peace with himself.

Rajasic attitude, which is generally recognized with colour red, is marked by excessive activity. *Rajasic* person is always anxious, restless and stressed. With single-minded pursuit of wealth, he wraps himself in endless greed, worries and anxieties. He runs after wealth and worldly enjoyments as if he is forced by insatiable demons. If he is a millionaire he craves to be multi-millionaire, and if he is multi-millionaire he desires to be billionaire. At times a *rajasic* person becomes so infatuated with high ambitions that he falls into the trap of undesirable means of accumulating wealth. The greed of such person increases to the extent that only the thing which is beyond his reach escapes his attention. He demands immediate results and his attitude of multiplying wealth becomes totally uncontrollable. A *rajasic* person works very hard to possess, to procreate and to protect. He is always worried and fearful of losing whatever he owns and constantly concerned about making more. His life becomes primarily devoted to pursuit of money and power. His field of activities is stretched almost out of proportion and he says, 'this wealth is mine and there will be more'.

Tamas, the dark inertia, is symbolized by black and navy blue. A *tamasic* person lives in a deluded world of total ignorance which is far beyond the realities of life. He is always confused and thinks that he is being destined to live by chance and not by choice. He acts very whimsically without any clear purpose and goal in mind. Even if he has the ability and capacity to achieve something; he does not make enough efforts. He keeps looking back at life and feels that somehow he missed everything. He feels bitter and depressed, regretting whatever has happened in the past. He also lacks discerning qualities and does not know how to make proper use of what he has.

There is a true incident from the life of an old woman who kept saving the money underneath the kitchen stove. She had thousands of dollars in her possession but still lived in utter poverty. At the time of death when she lost her voice, she kept pointing towards the stove, in order to tell her family about the hidden treasure. But nobody could understand anything. A few days after her death, her family found several bundles of dollars underneath the stove; those were half burnt and destroyed. A *tamasic* person lives his life in ignorance and dies in pain and ignorance. The human birth, instead of being an opportunity for spiritual growth and liberation, proves to be total waste for him and that constitutes the most tragic fall of human life.

Sri Kṛṣṇa tells Arjuna that these three qualities of conditioned-self become deeply rooted in the subtle levels of consciousness and accompany the individual as *samskaras* from one life to another. This processed information in mind determines the type of life one lives at present and also the life hereafter. He makes it clear to Arjuna, that life is not just locked in present; it is a continuity of thoughts and memories. The thoughts of today have received their continuation from those of yesterday and will express in the destiny of tomorrow. Every single thought of life is an extension of the past—seeking its expression into the actions of future. This continuity prevails throughout the life time and also continues even after death when the physical body perishes. He explains to Arjuna, that when a person leaves his body with the predominance of *Sattva* (purity) he attains the realms of the enlightened ones. He is generally born in a family of yogis who are spiritually awake and have experienced the highest truth. The *sattvic* attitude of his previous life guides him to pursue the path of spirituality and even if born in a rich, prosperous and royal family, he feels intuitively persuaded towards devotional love of God and service to humanity. He resumes the experiential knowledge of Supreme-Self and remains aligned with his pure, luminous, enlightened way of life. When a person leaves his body with the preponderance of passionate thoughts and *rajasic* tendencies, he is born among those who are attached to worldly enjoyments, and excessive activities. If the individual dies with the predominance of *tamasic* thoughts, he is born in a family of deluded and spiritually ignorant people. The vast disparity which we see among the species of the world clearly indicates the truth that every body comes to the world, wrapped with the shadows of conditioned nature. Every one checks in with some baggage of thoughts, memories and *samskaras* and also checks out with the baggage of memories, latencies and *samskaras* because of his added shopping in every life. The present life is indeed a preparation for the immediate next life and many more to come in the distant future.

Sri Krṣṇa alerts mankind about the subtle play of *gunas*

(qualities of mother nature) that initiate all kinds of activities in the world. These masks of nature, although quite distinct in their expression, still manifest themselves in coordination and cooperation with one another. The predominance of one can be observed in relation to the other two. A person becomes *sattvic* by consciously overpowering the *rajas* and *tamas*. When the *rajasic* tendency is expressed in the behaviour of an individual, the other two are partially dormant. Similarly, when the *tamasic* attitude dominates the personality of an individual, the *sattvic* and *rajasic* qualities become enshroud. Any tendency that overpowers suppressing others manifests its essentiality.

The realization of the presence of Supreme-Soul beyond the slavery of the conditioned behaviour is realized only when we are able to develop our conscious relationship with the Supreme-soul and realize the essentiality of our unconditioned nature. In unity with the pure luminous nature of the Self, we rise above the slavery of our conditioned behaviour and are liberated from false identifications and the masks of the conditioned-self.

After listening to the qualities of matter and how we become conditioned by them, Arjuna makes a request to know more about the lifestyle of that special person who lives above the slavery of his conditioned nature. Sri Kṛṣṇa explains that an enlightened person, who understands the games of mind and the tricks and treats of the conditioned behaviour, lives as a witness and master of his moods and inclinations. He is very intuitive and knows how to make the best use of every situation. Whether in war or in peace his clarity of vision about past, present and future is remarkable. He is intelligent, alert, organized and perpetually centred in the awareness of the Higher-Self. For example, when the *sattvic* bliss of Divine shines through his words and deeds, he does not get involved in vain discussions of scriptural philosophies. He never brags about his inner enlightenment and special psychic powers. Whenever someone appreciates him he takes every word of appreciation as an appreciation of the Lord within. He regards honour and dishonour, loss and gain, pleasure and pain, as only passing phases of life. For him all events are mere appearances and disappearances of ḳaleidoscopic dispositions. He lives as a master and controller of the triad in nature and manipulates the *gunas* according to his choice and need. When an impulse for action is awakened he accepts it as a call from the Supreme Lord and works for the welfare of humanity. He takes upon his plans and projects as God ordained work. A *sattvic* person ignores taking credits for the work well done and also does not regret at the failure of his attempt. He knows his limitations and understands exactly where his freedom lies and where bondage lies. Everyday is a new day for him. He knows clearly, that the life which we live is in the tissue of every day and every hour. The present moment is our most precious possession.

A *gunateeta* is not devoid of all the *gunas* (qualities of mother nature) of course his life is wrapped with the triad of nature but he is above and beyond the bondage of *gunas*. For him the slavery of *gunas* has become *atita*. Since he remains grounded in the bliss of the Supreme Brahman, he becomes a witness of his thoughts, words and deeds. He closely observes the silent play of *gunas* and remains totally unaffected by them. He is quite familiar with the life suppressing tricks of *tamas* as it sneaks in suppressing *sattva* and *rajas* he immediately becomes alert and does not let negligence and laziness make advances. He educates himself about living in the present, from moment to moment. He is also quite aware of the *rajasic* influences that generate insatiable desires for worldly enjoyments. He knows that popping up the thoughts of greed and jealousy in human mind are natural but the person's involvement is personal. A *gunateeta* who lives his life above and beyond the slavery of *gunas*, observes and monitors every little wisp of thought that passes through his mind. He beholds, perceives and acts only as a spectator. A liberated soul who is spontaneously settled in the serenity of the Supreme Self always remains balanced and detached maintaining a calm, peaceful equilibrium under all circumstances.

There is a very interesting incident from the life of Guru Gobind Sahib. Once the great Sikh teacher was sitting on the bank of a river and reading some holy scriptures; when Raghunath, a rich disciple proud of his wealth and status, came and presented him a pair of gold bangles studded with costly gems. Guru Gobind Sahib took one of them, held it in his hand and looked at the darting shafts of light from costly diamonds. Suddenly it slipped from his hand and rolled down the bank into the swift flowing water of the river. Raghunath screamed in frustration and jumped into the stream to catch the bangle. The great guru became absorbed again in readings from the Holy Scripture and the river grabbed quietly what it stole and languidly flowed on its way. It was late in the evening when the twilight faded across the horizon that Raghunath came back from the river, tired, exhausted, disappointed and wrapped in his own thoughts of great loss. He panted and requested the guru to tell him the exact direction in which the bangle rolled into the river. The great guru smiled and rolling the other bangle said, 'there it went'. This is what we call *gunateet sa uchate*—freedom of soul from the masks of conditioned-self. Perfect calmness, self mastery, total absence of ego, detachment and righteous actions characterize the life of a liberated soul. Guru Gobind Singh was a great saint, a great warrior and a great king who ruled his kingdom as an embodiment of Divine Himself.

Any person who remains grounded in the essential nature of the Divine and is constantly connected with the Lord in Yoga, surely attains a positive control over the slavery of his conditioned behaviour and the triad of the *gunas*. It is very important to remember that human life is a great gift of God. Human beings are blessed with subjective awareness of the Supreme-soul. Every person has the potential to experience the presence of God and receive sufficient guidance for self-realization and God-realization. Once again Sri Kṛṣṇa tells Arjuna about the necessity of undivided honest devotion to the Supreme Lord, which helps the person to remain perpetually aligned with the indwelling-Self and observe the play of *gunas* in day-to-day life. It is the devotional love of God and spiritual intimacy with Divine which nurtures *sattvic* qualities in life and opens the doorway for Divine knowledge, self analysis, inner wisdom, and self-improvement. It is the experiential knowledge of the Supreme-Soul which liberates a person from the bondage of his conditioned habits and brings a shift in awareness. The grace of the Divine is indeed spontaneously expressive. It is always there for us and within our reach. It only needs to be called with faith, love and devotion.

The Buddha and Sri Sankaracharya have not been chosen for the Lord's grace just randomly; they achieved the grace, through total surrender in God. They earned the grace by their own efforts, austerities, and unconditional love for the Divine. It is the duty of every person to prepare himself to be receptive to the call of the Divine with faith and sincere efforts. Grace of the Supreme Lord is not an exception to certain rules of caste, creed and nationality; the grace follows the eternal law of sincere efforts, determination, devotion, meditation and unconditional love for God.

It is only in human life that we get an opportunity for self-analysis, self-realization and liberation. It should be our endeavour to learn to live a life which is consciously connected with the Divine. Human life should become a means of self-realization and God-realization. As declared earlier by Sri Krsna *"uddhared atmanatmanam natmanam avasadayet atmaiva hy atmano bandhur atmaiva ripur atmanah*" which means 'let a man lift himself by his own Self; let him not degrade himself; for he himself is his own friend and he himself is his own enemy'.

Two birds closely associated and intimate friends, perch on the same tree. One is busy tasting the fruits while the other is simply watching and remains peaceful.

— Rigveda 1.164.20

8

Realization of the Supreme-Self

Bhagawad Geeta, Chapter 15
Purushottamayoga

Realization of the Supreme-Self is the *Purushottama* Yoga—going into yogic communion with the Supreme *Purusha* who is beyond all fields; and the knower of fields. It is the experiential knowledge of the unified field. It is an introduction to the Higher-Self. It is identification of the human-soul with the Supreme-Soul. It is being awakened into consciousness of the Supreme *Purusha (Brahmi-chetna).* Sri Kṛṣṇa opens the dialogue with the words *Urdhvamulamadhahsakham*—having its roots above and branches below, the tree of life is primordial. Earlier, Sri Kṛṣṇa has given an elaborate description of the field of experiences *(kshetra)* and also the knower of the field *(kshetrajña)* separately. Here He describes the field of experiences with the unique allegory of an *Aswattha* tree. *Aswattha* means "that which will not remain the same till tomorrow". It is perpetually changing, constantly growing and expanding in all directions. The roots of this tree are strongly entangled deep down in the world of mortals; nourished by actions and experiences. The roots represent the results of past actions, the branches, buds and drop down aerial roots represent the cycle of birth, death and rebirth going on ceaselessly. The expression *nanto na cadihr* stands for no beginning and no end in space or time. It has been declared as *avyayam* (eternal) by the knowers of truth. The roots of the tree are deeply soaked in the primordial principle of sempiternal urge to action. It is the involvement of pure consciousness in the mundane world as it becomes conditioned by the masks of nature and nurtures the flow of life in individual as well as in the universe. The tree with roots above and branches below has been mentioned by the scholars of *Kathopanishad.* Prof. Ranade also gives description of a similar type of tree in his writings. Its boughs with their buddings—events, things, catastrophes— stretch through all lands and times. Its boughs are histories of nations. Its rustle is the noise of human existence. It grows there, the breath of human passion rustling through it—It is *Igdrasil,* the Tree of Existence. It is the past, present and future". *Aswattha* also stands for the tree of banyan family which is constantly expanding by throwing the branches down into the ground that become roots again. The tree of *samsara,* which is the world of experiences, with its roots above in the Supreme consciousness, is the individual body as well as the cosmic body.

Roots upward means the life starts from the roots above that are settled in the *Brahmarandhra* in the form of thoughts, latencies and *samskaras.* Life is an expression of information fed by the software of memories in the *Brahmarandhra.* The seat of *Brahaman* is in the *Brahmarandhra* (the crown of the head) from where the entire body is nourished and sustained. At the time when a baby is conceived, it is in the *Brahmarandhra,* where consciousness gets seated. At that time the thought of the mother, that of the father and thoughts of the incoming soul, enter together as one uniform thought into consciousness of the mother. This triple combination of thoughts and *samskaras* expresses itself into a unique personality. Each and every life is nearly the expression of some thoughts, memories and latencies. So it is quite clear that the roots of life are the memories enclosed in mind. Mind is conditioned energy which keeps revolving from one life to another until it becomes silent and goes into realization of the Supreme-Self.

Power of *karma* presides over the entire course of life. Every single moment in life has been pre-designed to some extent, such as happiness, unhappiness, suffering and blessings, appear and disappear in a certain order. It is true that the conditioned behaviour enclosed in the memories of the past expresses itself in the form of destiny. Every person is born with a free will to think and work— the way he wants; but he is surely bound to go through the result of his each and every thought and action. *Karmas* are indeed the root of *samsara*. Various thoughts, actions and activities of life are various roots that constantly nourish the tree of life. The *karmas* create bondage to hopes, dreams, and memories in the form of *samskara* and provide momentum to the cycle of birth, death and rebirth. The world is a vast field of actions. Everybody inherits, from his previous existence and conforms to the law of cause and effects. In the words of Maharishi Mahesh Yogi, "The wheel of karma keeps on creating, evolving, and dissolving the phenomenal creation in cycles of existence and nonexistence of the cosmos as a whole, and the individual finds his share in it as a part of it".

Sri Kṛṣṇa tells Arjuna that understanding the tree of *samsara* is very difficult. It is the manifestation of various interconnected events. It is too difficult to trace its origin because every single root comes from the preceding one. We can see clearly that history of the entire universe is the evolutionary chain of alterations which is being worked out by a specific law of *karma* (cause and effect). The entire process is a constant and orderly flow of birth, death, and rebirth. Everybody and everything has its heritage in the One which existed before. Understanding the law of *karma* is very difficult as long as we are involved in the pursuit of material comforts. Sri Kṛṣṇa tells us to wake up from the circular patterns of conditioned thinking and comprehend the truth, behind the perceptual boundaries of the senses. He repeats the *Upanishadic* message: arise, awake and achieve which is yours. He declares that human beings are not just passive victims of some unknown destiny. Every person has the ability and strength to improve the quality of life and be liberated from the bonds of *karmas*. Sri Kṛṣṇa says—*asangastrena drdhena chittva* which means cut the deep rooted tree with the strong axe of non-attachment. The roots of this tree of *samsara* are covered by the feeling of 'I and Mine'. The 'I-Ness' has to be replaced by 'Thou and Thine', with total surrender in God. It is a fact that our bondage is in our identification with the ego that gives us the feeling of 'I and Mine'. It deludes our vision and makes it very narrow and selfish. Ego cries for name and fame. For example, when everything goes our way and we achieve recognition, our ego expands but if things don't move the way we want, we often blame others, sometimes even God.

In a state of disappointment and frustration, our vision becomes narrow and selfish. An arrogant person struggles constantly and tries to prove to others that he is better, more educated and wealthy. He brags a lot about his achievements and lives in a world of his own self-imagined importance. Since he expects and demands attention from others he usually becomes deprived of genuine love of others. He generally becomes fearful, lonely, and lives in miserable bondage. Demanding to be noticed, loved and respected, is the wailing cry of a heart bound by the strong fetters of ego. As Dr. Paul Brunton writes, "in delusions of the ego, and in its ignorance of true nature behind, that which expresses itself in the personal and vertical Pronoun 'I', are the source, both of the evil it does and the ignorance it shows. In its unchecked selfishness is mankind's worst advisor."

In order to overcome the pressure of ego, we can make some changes in our thought process with the help of *Mantra jaap*. With constant repetition of *Mantra*, our identification with God becomes natural and slowly our identification with ego starts fading. As soon as the thick veil of ego is lifted, we are awakened into a specific level of enlightened awareness where dispassion and detachment from the mundane world takes place and we are liberated from egoistic conditioned memory. The anchorage with the Supreme Self replaces the erroneous egocentric ideas with relaxed, flawless thinking.

I like these words of John Blofield. He says : "complete negation of the ego, conscious union with the source of the being is a task so hard to accomplish within one life time that not a moment may be wasted; for if the opportunity is missed who knows how many life time must elapse before the condition needed for further progress are encountered." He strongly believed in the spiritual momentum created by the constant repetition of mantra which could bring significant changes in our lives. It is indeed a fact that constant remembrance of God with undivided devotion connects our thoughts to the Supreme-Self, and disconnects our thoughts from the old dispositions.

Human life is a great blessing of the Divine. Human

beings are blessed with subjective awareness and can perceive the presence of God. Human beings are free and independent in the performance of their actions. Every individual has the ability to make and chart his own destiny. Swami Vivekananda has written that '*karma* is the eternal assertion of human freedom'. Between *bhagya* and *Bhagavan* i.e. destiny and God, there is something we have within our control and that is how we perform our actions. Every person is absolutely free in performance of actions but bound in reaping the fruits thereof. This reminds me of some beautiful lines by Omar Khayyam, "I sent my Soul through the Invisible, Some letter of that After-life to spell : And by and by my soul returned to me, And answered, I Myself am Heav'n and hell :" A person encloses himself into the web of bondage in human life; but at the same time it is only in human life wherein he can liberate himself from the bondage. *Moksha* or liberation is within the access of every human being. It becomes distant and difficult to experience because of our own ignorance and negligence. When we take refuge in Supreme Divinity with unflinching faith and love, we are awakened to the purity of the Supreme-Self and live a life inspired by the unified field of transcendental unity which brings spontaneous detachment from the worldly enjoyments.

After presenting a detailed description of *samsara,* Sri Kṛṣṇa tells Arjuna about the essential nature of *jivatma.* The word *jiva* comes from the Sanskrit word *jiv* means 'to breathe'. *Jivatma* means a fragment of *atma* who identifies with *jiva.* *Jivatma* is essentially one with *Atman*—the Supreme-Soul but also distinct because of its separate assumed identity which is enclosed in personal thoughts and *samskaras.* *Paramatma* is the eternal reality behind the mask of *jivatma.* The Supreme-soul is the essentiality of everything; it is the invisible thread which connects every thing and every body in the entire creation with one another. Just as gold is considered to be the reality in all types of gold ornaments, just as water is considered to be the reality in bubbles, waves and tides, similarly, the Supreme consciousness is the only reality of whatever appears to be manifested in the world. As a bubble of water from ocean appears to be separate because of air in it, similarly the individual-soul appears to be separate from Supreme-soul because of its assumed identity with the body. Pure consciousness appears different in its manifestations because of the limitations and conditions around it. Individual life is a wave which emerges from the wholeness of pure consciousness without disturbing its peace and serenity.

The processes of creation, evolution and dissolution are the diverse expressions of Supreme-spirit. In essence, the embodied-soul is identical with the universal-soul— the Supreme Brahman. An eternal fragment of the Supreme-Soul permeates everything in the world. This reminds me of this famous hymn from the Vedas, *"Aum purnamadah purnamidam purnata purnamudachyate, Purnasya purnnamadaya purnameva sisyate"* means That is whole, This is whole, whole comes out of whole; what is left, is also whole. Everything in the macrocosm as well as the microcosm declares the wholeness of the Supreme-soul. A seed becomes a tree and generates thousands of seeds. Each seed from the tree is complete it itself and has the potential to become a tree again. Similarly in our body when one cell splits into two nothing is lost; each cell is complete in itself. The universe emerges out of fullness, it is sustained by the fullness and into the fullness it goes back again.

Sri Krsna tells Arjuna, that the pure consciousness becomes individualized when it identifies itself with mind, body and ego. It gradually becomes involved in the enjoyments of body and forgets the real identity. In essence the Supreme Spirit *Sat-chit-anand,* is *drista*, means the silent witness. It is also called *bhokta* because of its identification of happiness with the enjoyments of the world through senses. There is an interesting description in the *Mundaka Upanisad* about two birds sitting on the branches of the same tree of life. One bird is always busy enjoying the fruits of the tree while the other is only watching. The one, who is involved in enjoyment of fruits, seems to be sometime happy and some other time very unhappy; he is confused and suffers. But the one who is simply watching and remains a silent witness, is always peaceful and free. The bird who is busy enjoying the fruits of the tree symbolizes the individual-soul—the *nara* who remains involved in the enjoyment of worldly pleasures and eventually becomes confused about the realities of life but the one who is simply watching is the Supreme-soul *Narayana* Himself. The latter remains a silent witness and free.

As a wave in the ocean is essentially a part of the ocean, the individualized-soul is eternally a part of the cosmic-soul. The experience of alienation occurs because of duality; but when the individual-soul goes in unity with the Supreme consciousness, from the gross to the subtlest realms of awareness, the embodied-soul resumes its true identity and feels a part of the Supreme-soul again. It is the experience of being restored to the wholeness of Divine and freedom from false identifications. As a matter of fact, everyone can experience this truth even in day-to-day life. In moments of pain and disappointments when the individual seeks help from the indwelling Supreme-soul, he feels altogether renewed and revitalized by the power of the indweller. This is exactly like going back to the source of life and being a part of the ever renewing flow of life. A person feels weak and helpless as long as he follows the instructions of his egoistic behaviour. Once he takes refuge in God, the Supreme power takes care of him. It is only through the grace of the Divine, that the individual is blessed with realization of his own essential nature and infinity of his inherent powers.

Identification of *jivatma* with *Paramatma* is in direct proportion to detachment from the masks of conditioned-self and attachment to the purity of the Supreme-Self. This is the experience of *Atmabodha*—inner enlightenment. As long as the individual-soul holds tight to its false, separate and conditioned egoistic individuality, the person becomes bound to move along the guidance of his conditioned nature. But the moment he goes in unity with the Supreme-soul he becomes introduced to his Divine nature and moves step by step towards the realization of his true identity as the Supreme Spirit. It is being awakened to one's own completeness.

Swami Vivekananda says, "Each soul is potentially divine". The real nature of *jivatma* is *Sat-chit-Ananda*. In this connection Swamiji has given a very good example, 'Once a tigress attacked a flock of sheep. As she jumped, she gave birth to a cub and died. The cub was raised in the company of sheep. As the sheep bleated, so did the cub. One day a tiger attacked the same flock of sheep and was totally amazed to see another tiger roaming around with the flock of sheep. When the wild tiger attacked, the cub began to bleat. The wild tiger dragged the cub to the water pond and roared : look at your face in the water. It is just like mine. In the beginning it was difficult for the cub to understand but quickly the cub realized the identical voice and roared to the full strength and felt very good about its true identification". Similarly, the Supreme-Soul keeps reminding us of our essential nature and identity. Whenever we accelerate ourselves to a specific level of consciousness we are introduced to our essentiality as the Supreme *Purusha,* the master of the universe. Sometimes we are blessed with the realization of the Self through the help of saints and sages that help us eliminate our *jiva-brahma-bheda bhranti* in the form of inner awakening into the field of pure consciousness.

The self-imposed identity of the individualized soul with the mind is very strong; it follows the individual from one life to another. *Jivatma* remains united with the faculty of sensory perceptions, thoughts and impressions throughout the lifetime and also leaves the physical body with their repositories as the breeze carries the fragrance of the flowers. *Jivatma* packs up all the information of mind and senses while leaving the physical body and also enters into another body with the package. The individual soul goes from one body to another, forced by the residual impressions accumulated during the life time; and also retains its individuality from one life to another. Although in general, people consciously forget about their past lives, but still the latent memories from their previous life guide them into new actions in present life.

The Doctrine of Reincarnation is not only a theory of the ancient seers and sages, even modern psychologists have started showing an increased interest in the phenomenon of life hereafter. Many psychiatrists around the world have given descriptions of specific case histories in which some unusual behaviour occurs in early years of life which is definitely suggestive of reincarnation. Dr. Ian Stevenson, a great psychologist of Canada, has given high credibility to the theory of rebirth. He describes several case histories in his famous book *20 Cases Suggestive of Reincarnation*. The case history of Mrs. Swarnalatha Mishra who could recall two earlier lives at the age of ten is really interesting. Although in her present life Swarnalata was raised in a Hindi-speaking family, but some of her favourite poems and songs apparently belonged to the traditions from Bengal. While describing about her past two lives, Swaranlata told the doctor that she lived one of her previous life in Katni which is about hundred miles from her present home in Panna; and the other one in Sylhet which is now in Bangladesh. Dr. Ian writes that this young woman's case provides some of the strongest evidence for the theory of reincarnation ever found in this field. The journey of the soul is ever renewing on the path of eternity. Dr. Radhakrishnan, the great philosopher and educationist, also describes in his book *An Idealist View of Life* that the theory of rebirth is more reasonable than the denial of rebirth. The doctrine of reincarnation has been accepted even outside India by the great educationists like Pythagoras, Plato, Empedocles and later by Plotinus and the Neo–Platonists. Among the Muslims we see some examples given by Sufi writers and among Hebrews by the writers of Kabbala. It has been mentioned by Bruno, Von Helmont, Swedenborg, Lessing, Herder and

MacTaggart.

Sri Kṛṣṇa has been explaining in detail to Arjuna that every embodied-soul enters into new life with residual of *samskaras* (memories) and also leaves the body wrapped with new *samskaras* accumulated during the entire span of life. At the time of death soul leaves one body and goes into another wrapped with the conception for the future body in the form of most favourite thoughts and memories. Each new life is an expression of some memories of past lives. For example, just reflect on the span of present life till today. It exists only in the form of some thoughts; that have gone into the memory bank and have become merely a memory of yesterday. All cherished moments of life, strong urges and desires, difficult times, favourable times— where are they? The entire past has become a mere idea of mind. The entire life is a series of thoughts preordained in a certain order and the cycle of transmigration is also a series of thoughts which appear and disappear constantly tumbling over one another. The memory bank is created, maintained and sustained by the individual-soul. Each and every thought remains alive because of the conscious involvement of the embodied-soul with it. Every individualized soul takes upon new life bound by its own *karma*. Every individual-soul is independent in choosing parents, spouse and friends. We don't meet people just by chance. Every moment in life rolls in a certain pre-designed pattern. Each and every person moves alone on the path of eternity with a certain goal in mind.

Sri Kṛṣṇa tells Arjuna that involvement of the soul with mind and body is not realized by people in general and that is why they live in bondage and die in bondage. They experience good and bad times under the spell of sensory enjoyments. Every single moment in life expresses sufficient reasons of bondage and slavery but hardly anyone comprehends the real cause of slavery. People live in ignorance without realizing their in-born potential and perennial connection with the Supreme-Self. Sri Kṛṣṇa mentions once again, *"utkramantam sthitam vapi bhunjanam va gunanvitam vimudha nanupasyanti pasyanti jnanacaksusah"*—means the transcendental majesty of the Divine is definitely missed by ignorant people but it is distinctly perceived by men of wisdom who constantly live in the awareness of the Supreme-self. They have the insight and ability to experience the soul as the knower of the body and make proper efforts for self-realization and God-realization. The phenomenon of something emerging and disappearing is visible and deeply structured in our consciousness. The silent observer who is witnessing the entire process is not perceived by people in general, but the yogi who is perpetually tuned to the higher state of awareness remains in touch with the silent onlooker and enjoys the silent communion from moment to moment. Success in spirituality is accomplished by some dedicated, sincere, pure-hearted and fully committed individuals. An aspirant who aims at self-realization has to be fully resolved, genuinely inquisitive, intuitive and diligent. Spiritual progress demands proper endeavour made through the purity of mind, and the clarity of intelligence. The yogis who have experienced and perceived the Supreme-soul in yogic unity and are constantly making efforts to maintain that connectedness, are definitely liberated from the false identifications.

With reference to realization of the Supreme *Purusha,* Sri Kṛṣṇa draws Arjuna's attention from the cosmic body to the human body and says : *'Sarvasya caham hrdi sannivisto mattah smrtir jnanamapohanam ca'* means 'I am seated in the hearts of all. I am the source of memory, knowledge and reason'. Although the Supreme consciousness is the essence of life and resides in each and every little molecule of the body but it can be perceived, intimated and experienced only at the heart centre. Realization of the Supreme Lord at the shrine of the heart is easy and most rewarding experience of life. It is easy because the individual is not seeking something distant, not something foreign and alien; it is very much known, familiar and one's own indwelling-self.

Contemplation at the heart centre has been highly recommended in almost all the religious traditions of the world. The spiritual experience of proximity with the Divine at the heart centre prepares the person for the devotional love of God. It is at the shrine of the heart where the psychological and spiritual transformation takes place. The person is enlightened and becomes the embodiment of Divine bliss. *Upanisads* have declared gloriously *Hridyaantar jyoti*—means the light at the shrine of the heart, *Hridyaguha* means the cave of the heart where the indweller *(antaryami)* resides and *pranavam iswaram vidat sarvesyehriti sansitam,* means experience the presence of the Supreme Lord seated in the hearts of all. In the Bible also there is a similar type of description by St. Marcus— there in the heart dwells the Lord in His kingdom. It is indeed in the subtle realms of consciousness at the *anahat chakra* where the aspirant can perceive and experience the presence of the spirit within. When an ardent devotee concentrates at the heart centre and makes effort to grasp the sound waves of the eternal *nada (aum),* he goes into yogic unity with the indwelling-soul. Every person in the world is born with a natural intimacy with the Divine at the heart centre, but as we grow older we lose our conscious connection and forget about our mutual relationship with God at the shrine of the heart. Concentration on the sound of holy syllable *Aum* at the temple of heart brings back the memory of our primordial relationship with the source of life and helps us to recognize and experience our closeness with the Divine.

Meditation on the sound of holy syllable is a progressive realization of the Self and unity in transcendence. It is a gradual process of going in yogic unity and remaining aware of our proximity with Divine. In the initial stages of practice, intimacy with Lord is established by merely repeating the mystic syllable at the conscious levels of awareness. Second is *madhyama* when the sound and meaning of *Aum* are settled in the depth of increased awareness and we become conscious of silence between two successive syllables. Catching this silence in the gap leads to profound concentration. The third is *pashyanti* when the meditator simply listens to the celestial sound and remains aware of it. The sound becomes endowed with enormous spiritual power and vibrates through the entire body. The fourth is the *para* when the human soul goes in unity with the cosmic soul. It is Being-Becoming and Bliss. This reminds me of some beautiful lines by Rabindranath Tagore, "Open the inner door of the shrine, light the candle, and let us meet there, in silence before our God". The joy of spiritual intimacy, the ecstasy of Divine love is known only to those who have experienced the presence of the Supreme in *hridaya kosha*.

The *Purushottama* yoga is the ultimate identification of the individual-soul with the Supreme-soul. It is the realization of the *uttamapurusha* (Higher-Self) within, which goes beyond the mutable and immutable. Realization of transcendent Self, the *uttamapurusha*, is being awakened into heightened awareness when the individual soul enters into the unified field of superconsciousness and actually becomes a witness of both the field and the knower of the field. As discussed earlier by Sri Krsna, there are two expressive aspects of Supreme-being in the world, the perishable which is changing every second of life, and the imperishable which enters into everything and makes that a potential living being. Every expression of life is the manifestation of Supreme spirit. To make it clearer we can say that there are two aspects of one Supreme Being. The perishable which is composed of five basic elements— fire, air, ether, earth and water, and includes all animate and inanimate. Although the predominance of these basic elements in nature—*panch mahabhuta,* differs in human beings and other species like trees, plants and other varieties in creation, but everything comes into existence evolving around these *panch mahabhutas*—energized by the Supreme-being which is imperishable and exists even when the entire universe perishes. The whole universe comes into existence from the Supreme spirit and eventually merges into the Supreme spirit. Everything in the universe comes into existence, sustains for a while and eventually dissolves to be born again because of the conscious involvement of the conditioned spirit with it. Sri Kṛṣṇa has explained earlier that the eternal *ansha*—fragment of the imperishable—becomes individualized conditioned soul because of its affinity for the physical, subtle and causal body.

The embodied-soul accepts this affinity in order to enjoy the comforts of the material world which leads to bondage of birth, death and rebirth. *Jivatma*—the specific, individualized, localized consciousness—is essentially the imperishable *Purusha*. The individual-soul is called *Purusha* in *Vedic* literature because it dwells in the city of physical body. *Puri* means city—the dwelling place and thus *purisayat* means who is resting in the body. Sri Kṛṣṇa tells Arjuna that the Supreme-being—*Uttamapurusha* transcends both the perishable and individualized, localized imperishable and yet permeates the entire universe. The Supreme spirit enters the three worlds (*triloka*)–the causal, astral and physical; maintains and sustains everything but still remains a silent witness. The Supreme consciousness which appears to be involved in all the changes of life is necessarily changeless, immutable and imperishable.

I like the way Dr. Radhakrishnan explains this, "the mutable as the changing universe, the immutable as the *mayashakti* or the power of the Lord and the Supreme is said to be eternal, pure, luminous and free from the limitations of the mutable and immutable". The transcendental-self is beyond *bhoor bhuvah swah*—means the physical-self, psychological-self, and embodied spiritual self, transcends all the realms of experiences and also the flow of time in which all activities take place. For example, during sleep when the physical body is at rest and the subtle body is active, the transcendent being observes all activities of the individual-soul; the experience of a person's involvement in dream and also the experience of peace and tranquillity in deep sleep when the physical body and subtle body both are at rest. Even in deep sleep when the individual-soul goes in unity with the source of life, the entire process is witnessed by the Supreme-soul. *Uttamapurusha*—the pure consciousness is the only power that gives validity to all experiences of waking, dream, and deep sleep. Sri Kṛṣṇa tells Arjuna to look behind the veil of his localized, individualized consciousness and experience the presence of silently witnessing Supreme *Purusha* who upholds the infinite dynamism of the entire universe. Sri Kṛṣṇa has used the word *sarvavit* for the enlightened yogi who knows how to enter into the subtle realms of infinite consciousness transcending the mind, body and conditioned spirit. *Sarvavit* literally means all-knower or *brahma jñani*. It is the most enlightened status in which the aspirant perceives the essential nature of both perishable and imperishable and goes beyond his limited self-assumed identity. The experience of unity in yogic communion eliminates all dualities, illusionary concepts and the individual perceives everything clearly and harmoniously.

It is not merely intellectual comprehension; it is the subjective apprehension of the Supreme *Purusha* that makes personal communion possible. Even a momentary experience of unity with the Supreme *Purusha* can change the entire course of life for the better. Sri Kṛṣṇa tells Arjuna that when the individual is awakened into the Blissful state of inner peace and tranquillity, his thoughts, words and deeds are constantly guided by the Divine will. He attains the state of cosmic consciousness and lives his life as an instrument in the hands of Divine. He appreciates and enjoys the proximity of the Supreme Lord, with genuinely aroused devotion and dedication. He worships the Lord from the very core of his heart and from the totality of his being. He feels peaceful, happy and exhilarated every minute of life. The echo of the inner unison helps him to maintain his devotional ecstasy. It keeps the covenants renewed perpetually. An aura of ineffable devotion and dedication prevails over his mind and the entire thinking faculty, which keeps him charged with the unique power of yogic communion. The joy of mutual intimacy with the Higher-self shows spontaneously in each and every word he speaks and every bit of work he performs. All duties of life are accomplished with renewed enthusiasm and also very effectively and successfully. An enlightened yogi lives his life in perpetual ecstasy of Supreme Bliss, and carries that Bliss along wherever he goes. He shares that Bliss with any one who comes across. The individual is blessed with inner peace, harmony and complete fulfilment.

The knowledge of the Supreme *Purusha* becomes revealed to us from the depth of our own awareness and from the field of pure consciousness. The inner wisdom and intuition expresses it in so many different ways, and helps us to solve the most difficult problems of life. Our love for God and respect for life blossoms in all respects. Let the grace of Lord be perceived by each and every one of us and become the means as well as the goal.

The holy syllable AUM is indeed the imperishable *Brahman* and the universe is the exposition of His glory. AUM is all what existed in the past, whatever is now and will be in future. AUM is the essence of everything around and everything is the manifestation of AUM.

— Mandukya Upnishad 1.1

9

The Field of Positive and Negative Forces
&
The Mysterious Power of Aum-Tat-Sat

Bhagawad Geeta, Chapter 16 & 17
Devasursampatti Vibhagayoga & Sraddhatriya Vibhagayoga

The Field of Positive and Negative Forces :

Sri Kṛṣṇa opens the dialogue and enlightens Arjuna about the field of positive and negative forces. He tells Arjuna about marked distinction between the *Devas* and the *Asuras* means gods and demons or the Divine and demonic characteristics of human nature. *Deva* literally means the one who knows how to give and share. The other word which is used for *Deva* is *Sura*. It is a Sanskrit word, which means the one who is consciously in tune with the Supreme-Self. *Asura* means the one who is not consciously in tune with the Supreme-soul. Sri

Kṛṣṇa opens the conversation with the words : *abhayam sattvasuddhir jñanayoga-vyavasthitih danam damas ca yajñas ca svadhyayastapa arjavam.* This means the Divine nature is marked by an acme of fearlessness, purity of heart, steadfastness in yogic knowledge, charity, performance of yajña, study of scriptures, austerity, modesty, straightforwardness, renunciation, humility, forgiveness, generosity, self-study, nonviolence, truthfulness, self-discipline, persistence, fortitude and universal love. The word *abhaya*—absolute fearlessness— is one of the most outstanding characteristic of the person who has learnt to live a life in perfect harmony with the Supreme-self. Fearlessness is a spontaneous expression of inner security and inner alignment with the Higher-self. Anyone who lives in unity with the source of life naturally lives in unity with the entire creation. He is very friendly, sincere, generous, secure, confident and fearless. He feels at home wherever he goes and creates an aura of friendliness all around. He wins the confidence of others and touches the heart of every one with his inner purity, inner security and honesty. Since he is secure and at ease with himself, he is at ease with others as well. His ideals are supportive of universal life. As a matter of fact, *abhaya, asanga,* and *ahimsa*—means fearlessness, detachment and nonviolence move hand in hand and do characterize an authentically spiritual person. Fearlessness, serenity and tranquillity of mind lead to *asanga* which means detachment, and detachment leads to nonviolence or universal love. A fearless person is indeed blessed and liberated—enjoys constant unity with the Supreme-Self.

This reminds me of some famous words from *Gitanjali* by the great poet Rabindranath Tagore: "Where the mind is without fear and the head is held high; Where the knowledge is free; Where the world has not been broken into fragments by narrow domestic walls; Where the words come out from the depth of truth; Where the tireless striving stretches its arms towards perfection; Where the clear stream of reason has not lost its way into the dreary desert sand of dead habit; Where the mind is led forward by thee into ever widening thought and action—into that heaven of freedom, my Father, let my country awake".

Purity of thoughts, words and deeds reflect the purity of Divine nature which is pure, unconditional and uncontaminated. People who are clean in mind and body are indeed the embodiment of Divine. In fact all spiritual disciplines such as *yajña*, worship, yoga, meditation, fasting, self-control focus on the purification of heart so that the light of the Higher-self can be perceived. It is the purity of Divine nature that brings people closer to each other in their original bond of spiritual intimacy. Purity of heart expresses itself as perpetual alignment with God. To accept the presence of Divine is one thing but to accept to live in the consciousness of the presence of Divine is what brings purification of heart. Blessed are those, who stay constantly aligned with the pure nature of Divine; they are walking manifestations of God.

People endowed with Divine nature are always steadfast in their pursuit of yogic unity with the indwelling Supreme-self. They know that yogic discipline is not only a religious practice. It is a necessity in order to live a healthy, wholesome, harmonious, peaceful, productive and useful life. It facilitates proper flow of *prana* or vital life energy through different levels of consciousness which improves efficiency, flexibility, resilience, endurance and stamina. Yogic unity in transcendence creates spiritual force for the person and adds emotional equanimity and balance in his life style. It is radiant and shines through the daily activities of life. It integrates almost every aspect of our personality and initiates us into living a successful prosperous, healthy life which is in harmony with the laws of Dharma.

After fearlessness, purity of heart and steadfastness in yogic discipline, the virtues such as *daya, dana, daman* have been discussed in detail. *Daya* is the quality of love and compassion for others and *dana* means charity. A person becomes compassionate and kind only when he learns to live in the awareness of the inner-self and feels himself reflected in others. Scriptures proclaim : *daya dharma ka mool hai* which means kindness and compassion form the basis of *Dharma*. The virtue of compassion brings people closer and binds them together with the feeling of love and care. A person can be regarded religious, only if his heart is full of compassion and kindness toward others. *Prajña* and *karuna* in fact move hand in hand. *Prajña* is increased awareness. It is conscious alignment with God and *karuna* is the virtue which is revealed through inner alignment with the source of life. *Daman* means self-control and self-discipline. With self control physical and psychological energy can be used in higher pursuits of self-realization and God-realization. *Daman* is a spiritual discipline and a necessity for all types of success, peace and harmony in life. *Yajña* means selfless service or sacrifice. *Yajña* is the initial step for yogic communication and communion. It is prayer-cum-contemplation which connects us at all the three levels of our existence—physical, psychological and spiritual. Offerings of purified butter and herbal mixture of medicinal plants in fire connects the individual to the material world and cosmic bodies; chanting of hymns with each offering brings alignment with the psychological and spiritual-self.

Nonviolence is one of the highest forms of austerity. Ancient sages have described the doctrine of nonviolence or *ahimsa* as *manase, vachya, karmana*—which means, do not hurt anybody by thought, word and deed. Every action which a person performs, and every word which he speaks, is the manifestation of a particular thought which has flashed in his mind. So even to think of harming others is an act of violence. Violence literally means violating the laws of the indwelling-Self, or going against the voice of the Self. So nonviolence is obedience to a higher law of *swadharma;* the voice of the indwelling-self.

Sri Krsna mentions truthfulness to be the most honourable virtue which helps us to develop many more virtuous habits. The habit of speaking truth is a great austerity. It keeps the person aligned with indwelling Divinity and gives a lot of inner strength, inner security and self-respect. It makes the person fearless and confident. All of us know how the great saint *Gautama* accepted *Satyakama Jabali* as his disciple simply because of his truthfulness. Speaking truth, promotes the harmony of thoughts, words and deeds and also improves our relationship with our own inner-self and with others. Speaking truth and taking pride in it, definitely reflects Divine nature which is pure and luminous. In the words of Gandhiji, "Truth is God and God is truth for us to experience. Be truthful and let the Absolute Truth be revealed to you. God is addressed as *Sat-chit-anand*, means Truth, awareness and bliss. Realization of truth leads us to increased awareness of the Self and awareness leads to Bliss. God combines all the three, that is why God is addressed as *Sat-chit-anand*. There should be Truth in thought, Truth in speech, and Truth in action. The man who has realized and actualized this Truth, for him, nothing else remains to be known, because all austerities are included in it. The pursuit of Truth is true *Bhakti* (devotion). It is the path that leads to God". The holy sages are truthful, pure and enlightened. They experience the presence of Divine at the shrine of their heart. The men of Divine nature are *Suras* who remain constantly in tune with the voice of Divine they spontaneously become interested in the study of the self at various levels of consciousness such as conditioned-self and the Supreme-self. They have the ability to examine the interaction of feelings and reason, to analyze their thoughts and emotions and negotiate with different circumstances of life adequately, peacefully, with wisdom and proper insight. Study of the self is the most rewarding gift of life.

Sri Kṛṣṇa gives a long lecture about Divine qualities and the demonic he has touched very briefly. He knows human psychology, and has made the most appropriate use of each and every word. He knows that it is a natural desire in human beings to listen about the good qualities at first and then the rest. By adopting good qualities with receptive attitude, we can easily abandon bad qualities. He tells Arjuna that Divine endowments help people to live in peace and harmony with their own inner-self, with others and with cosmic powers. These qualities are conducive to liberation and salvation while the demonic nature becomes the cause of suffering and bondage.

Sri Kṛṣṇa declares *dvau bhutsargau loke,* that is there are two types of people in this world, the divine and the demonic, the *Deva* and the *Asura.* Although every individual-soul *(Jivatma)* is potentially divine and a fragment of the Supreme-soul; but when the soul takes upon the human body, it is possessed with two strong desires. The individual-soul likes to enjoy everything in the material world; but being a fragment of the Divine, the soul feels comforted in closeness with the Supreme-Soul. In human body the soul *(jivatma)* becomes confused about mixed identities. Spiritual impulses give peace and harmony, while the primitive impulses create restlessness and confusion. Every person has the potential to rise in spirituality and work in copartnership with God but if he becomes a slave of his conditioned behaviour, he falls. A person can become the glory of the universe and also its ridicule. He can become the crown of creation, but if he acts against the voice of the Supreme-self, he becomes the scandal of the world. Although every person is essentially spiritual, but the degree of spiritual awareness differs from one person to another. In general, people are divided into two categories : men of divine qualities and those of demoniac qualities (The *Devas* and the *Asuras*). This statement of Sri Kṛṣṇa has been also echoed by Viktor Frankl in his book *Man's Search for Meaning*. He writes, "There are two races of men in the world, but only these two—the race of a decent man and the race of the indecent man. Both are found everywhere. No group consists entirely of decent or indecent people". This distinction is quite primordial. The old scriptures of India and other religious books of the world have described constant struggle between the gods and their deluded opponents. The master of light and the children of darkness, the celestial and the non-celestial, the good and evil. The Zoroastrian religious scriptures are full of tales, which illustrate war between the lower and higher forces. The story of the *Ramayana* also describes the conflict between *Devas* and *Asuras*.

In description of the demonic nature Sri Kṛṣṇa tells Arjuna that the deluded people cannot see the difference between the right and wrong. The concept of purity, good conduct, truthfulness and cleanliness does not exist for them. These people are consciously or unconsciously disconnected with the voice of the indwelling self and do heinous crimes in order to satisfy their passionate desires. The day-to-day dealings of these people are selfish and against the laws of *swadharma*. They involve themselves in harmful dealings with others, and create problems for themselves and for society. They take pride in cheating, and taking advantage of innocent people. For them the gratification of their personal desires is the highest goal in life. They lack manners and humility. These self-conceited people do not treat others with respect and reverence. They make fun of the religious ceremonies and even hesitate to salute the spiritual teachers, monks and elders. For these people of demonic nature, personal hygiene, cleanliness and the concept of integrated community living carries no meaning. They pollute the waterways and lakes with harmful waste, destroy the forests for selfish reasons.

Speaking about the problem of radio-active wastes of nuclear reactors in modern societies, E.F. Schumacher says, "No degree of prosperity could justify the accumulation of large amounts of highly toxic substance which nobody knows how to make "safe", and which remains an incalculable danger to the whole of creation for historical or even geological ages. To do such a thing is a transgression against life itself, a transgression infinitely more serious than any crime ever perpetrated by men. The idea that a civilization could sustain itself on the basis of such a transgression is an ethical, spiritual, and metaphysical monstrosity. It means conducting the economic affairs of man as if people really did not matter at all".

After giving a description of the Divine and demonic qualities of human beings, Sri Krsna declares desire, anger and greed to be the triple gates of hell; that bring about the downfall of the individual-soul. These Hi-three in human behaviour act in close copartnership with each other and do appear as uninvited friends.

The same concept has been discussed earlier in the dialogue, where Arjuna asks the question, "O' Krsna, by what a man is compelled to commit sin, as if driven by force, even against his will?" Sri Krsna says *kama yesha krodh yesha rajo guna samathbhava*—"O'Arjuna it is indeed the passionate desire, that goes into anger, which is the most vicious enemy of man". The person who is driven by passionate desires constantly lives under the impulse of acquiring, accumulating and possessing everything within his reach, or even something beyond his apprehension. He becomes a helpless victim of greed, and any obstacle and interruption in his plans causes frustration and anger. An angry man is forced into violence, retaliation and other sinful activities. 'Desire, anger and greed' together corrupt thinking faculty and become the cause of many day-to-day problems of life.

Victory over these three gates of hell brings enlightenment and liberation. When the darkness of ignorance is removed with the light of knowledge, the individual moves step by step towards the journey of self-realization and God-realization. This is called progressive realization, moving from less awareness to increased awareness and from bondage to freedom.

Sri Kṛṣṇa glorifies the knowledge of the Holy Scriptures and speaks about the need of scriptural knowledge in life. Human nature is notorious. The ancient *rishis* knew it very well. That is why they wrote the holy scriptures from their own subjective experience of the cosmic self, so that people can be guided into code of ethics and live a life in harmony with the voice of God. The holy scriptures do provide the most experienced and recognized guidelines to the individual with sufficient information. Knowledge of ancient holy books should be used for guidance in order to live a balanced and harmonious life. The study of the holy books purifies the individual and provides guidance for living a peaceful life which is in harmony with his own indwelling pure luminous self, with nature and the society in which he lives.

These holy scriptures are a great blessing to humanity given by the holy sages. These sacred books have been written on the basis of the *jñan, vijñan,* and *prajña—means* the knowledge, experiential knowledge, and the knowledge of yogic unity in transcendence. The knowledge of the sacred scriptures provides stability, integrity, sanctity and the concept of morality. The genuine progress of any society depends upon the fact, as to how much people rely upon the wisdom of the ancient books, in relation to the activities of their day-to-day life. The family and society where people lose their touch with the teachings of the scriptures, they live in utter confusion. The ethical religious traditions are incentives for harmonious living. The code of conduct helps the individual to follow the path of virtue, morality and primordial dharma. Therefore let the teachings of the ancient holy scriptures be the authority for determining the course of our activities from moment to moment. Every human being must follow the instructions of the scriptures at every step in life, until he becomes fully tuned to the voice of the Supreme-Self.

Sri Kṛṣṇa concludes that in order to live a harmonious life at the individual level as well as the member of a family and society, it is indeed the *swadharma* of mankind to remain conscious of the divine qualities by staying in touch with the voice of the Supreme-Self.

The Mysterious Power of Aum-Tat-Sat :

The dialogue becomes interesting when Arjuna continues to inquire regarding the mysterious power of faith and *Aum-Tat-Sat*. He wants to know more about *shradha* or faith. Sri Kṛṣṇa explains that faith is threefold: the *sattvic* (pure), the *rajasic* (passionate) and the *tamasic* means rooted in ignorance. All personal concepts, ideas, thoughts and activities of a person revolve around the type of faith he holds. "As a man's faith is, so is he". The quality of faith reflects the conditioned nature or *swabhava* of a person. *Swabhava* is the word that explains itself. *Swa* means the indwelling light and *bhava* means the personal conditioned thinking. So *swabhava* means personal thinking. He tells Arjuna that in general people are guided by three inherent qualities of nature, and divide themselves in three types—*sattvic* (pure), *rajasic* (passionate) and *tamasic* (ignorant).

The *sattvic* people are spiritually awake and enlightened. A *sattvic* person worships as a duty and makes offerings to the gods and goddesses without any desire for reward. For him, love of God and living a life in a most intimate relationship with God is everything. A man of clarity and genuine austerity, performs *yajñas*, chants hymns, studies scriptures, listens to the holy sermons, observes fasts, practices meditation and makes offerings only as a gesture of his personal duty towards the creation of the Lord. He perfectly understands the necessity of living in harmony with his inner-self, and with other fellow beings on the planet. He genuinely knows that each and every individual is indeed a very important member of the community, country and the world. Every one should understand his duties as well as his rights in order to live a peaceful, balanced and harmonious life.

He understands his duty and seeks orderliness in every work he performs. His attitude is enlightened and supportive of universal life. On the other hand, a *rajasic* person worships God in order to seek boons and bounties. His act of charity shows his hidden desire for name and fame. He is generally preoccupied with the worries of rewards even at the time when service is being offered. He makes offerings not for the sake of duty or appreciation for the blessings of God, but merely as an act of ostentation. While giving charities, his aim is to satisfy his ego by showing off his wealth, riches and resources. He performs all kinds of *yajñas* in order to earn more wealth, material comforts and respectable status in community. Sri Kṛṣṇa tells Arjuna that the *yajña* which is performed with a desire to gain something in return is *rajasic* (passionate). Any worship which is undertaken with a selfish personal motive is surely considered to be *rajasic;* instead of bringing peace and harmony, it brings anxiety, restlessness and bondage. The *rajasic yajña,* even though it is performed according to scriptures, contributes very little towards the goal of self-realization and liberation.

About the *tamasic* worship Sri Krṣṇa tells that it is generally performed out of fear and superstition. A *tamasic* worship is never in conformity with the ordinances of the sacred books. Sri Krṣṇa has also used the word *sraddhavirahitam* which literally means the service which is devoid of faith, respect and reverence, and which is performed with arrogance, hypocrisy, and for ostentation only.

The worship in which the Vedic hymns are not chanted whole-heartedly and the contribution (*dakshina)* is not made with respect, is definitely *tamasic.* In performance of *tamasic* worship the person does not get much peace and happiness, neither here or hereafter. He rather lives in constant guilt and shame.

With reference to the different types of austerities Sri Krṣṇa tells Arjuna that people, who practice violent austerities, torture their bodies and also hurt Me, who lives in the body. These ignorant people engage themselves in the practice of difficult austerities, which are against the laws of *swadharma*. They believe that mortification of the body is an austerity and torture their bodies in order to get the attention of other people.

Sri Krsna makes it clear to Arjuna that self-discipline and self-control should not be confused with the physical torture of the body. The practice of self-mortification is painful and unworthy; it should not be followed at all.

He also enlightens about three kinds of austerities for self-purification, self-realization, and God-realization. For example, the austerity of body includes worship of the gods and goddesses, respect of learned Brahmins and spiritual teachers; practice of self-discipline, inner purity, celibacy and nonviolence. Living a life which is in perfect harmony with the cosmic forces is indeed the worship of gods and goddesses. Here the person is blessed with full cooperation and support of nature in return.

In regards to the austerity of body, Sri Krsna mentions about *Brahmacarya* means *brahma-acharan* means purity of thoughts, words and deeds and also respecting the vows of celibacy. Nonviolence as discussed earlier means not violating the voice of the indwelling-self. It is a state of perfect peace and harmony with Supreme-self and with others. The holy scriptures declare *ahimsa parmo dharma* means nonviolence is the first and foremost *Dharma* of mankind.

After the austerity of physical body, Sri Kṛṣṇa tells Arjuna about the austerity of speech. Speaking appropriate words with the knowledge of how to speak, what to speak, when to speak and how much to speak, is the austerity of speech. Speaking truth is an austerity, which makes us fearless, and secure. It gives self-respect and self-confidence. On the other hand, the people who tell lies lack self-confidence, self-respect and self-reliance. They become the victim of bad habits and harm themselves more than anybody else. The person, who tells lies, becomes fearful and suspicious because he remains under the impression that others are also lying. The person who is always suspicious does not trust others; he lives in conflict with himself and with everybody else. About this I like to quote these lines by Emerson, "Men suffer all their life under the foolish superstition, that they can be cheated. But it is as impossible for a man to be cheated by any body else but himself". Speaking truth, and taking pride in it, is indeed an austerity. Truthfulness in thoughts, words and deeds is genuine devotion to God. It purifies the individual and gives him inner strength and stability. The famous words from the *Bible,* "nothing gives me greater joy than to hear that my children live in truth".

Describing austerity of mind Sri Kṛṣṇa says *maunam atmavinigraha* which means the silence of mind and self-discipline. *Maunam* is the silence of mind and speech. *Mauni* or *muni* is the one who has learnt to live in the silence of the Supreme-Self. Silence of speech promotes silence of thoughts and silence of mind. It gives an opportunity to experience the silence of the Supreme-Self in yogic unity. The *mauna vrata* gives an experience of deep relaxation. It gives peace of mind, and an opportunity for self-study. In silence we are aligned to the source of life and are introduced to the essential nature of the Self which is pure and unconditioned. It is indeed a blissful experience.

In detailed explanation of different austerities Sri Kṛṣṇa draws Arjuna's attention to the importance of the quality of food we eat. In general, there are three types food consumed by people. The food which promotes longevity, purity, strength, health, happiness, and good-appetite is *sattvic* means pure. The milk and milk products, vegetables, fruits, wheat, barley, rice, almonds, etc., come under the category of *sattvic* food. The kind of food that are bitter, pungent and dry are liked by *rajasic* and the food which is fermented and stale is liked by *tamasic* people. This also includes non-vegetarian food which has been considered totally unfit for human body. Human teeth are meant for eating vegetarian food; and also human intestine which is long and narrow is not designed to digest any type of meat.

The physical body is called the *anamaya kosa* which has a direct relation with *manomaya kosa, pranmaya kosa, vigyanmaya kosa* and *anandmaya kosa*. These various fields are interconnected and work in unison with each other. To experience unity with the Self, the journey starts from physical body which is *anamaya kosa*. The food is called '*anna*' in Sanskrit. *Anna* is related to *prana*—the life breath. *Prana*—is very closely connected with *mana* the mind. *Shruti Bhagwati* describes at length *"Jaisa khave anna, vaisa hove mana"*—means the quality of thoughts is controlled directly by the quality of food we eat. *Chandogya Upanishad* describes that the food we eat, is digested in a threefold process. The coarsest portion becomes the faces; the middle becomes flesh and subtlest becomes the mind. So it is very important to eat the specific quality of food which promotes purity of thoughts. Besides, it is not just the ingredients of the food which matters but also the way it is cooked and consumed makes a big difference. For example, when a certain recipe is given to five cooks, the results are always different, because each one of them adds his own thoughts and feelings into the cooking. Good and positive thoughts in cooking do produce pleasant and enjoyable taste.

Apart from the choice of right quality of food, it is also important to remember the appropriate means of livelihood. The food earned through appropriate and inappropriate means of livelihood does produce the negative and positive influence respectively on our thinking faculty. A prayer before eating the meal has been highly recommended in almost all religious books of the world. The humble words of gratitude, such as, Thank you God for the world so sweet, Thank you God for the food we eat, aligns the mind and body to the source of life. The prayer is asking for grace and blessing which brings a relaxed flow of awareness in mind and helps the body in the proper digestion of food. It is really important to eat the meal in a prayful mood and remain silent and relaxed while eating, or have good, pleasant conversation with others at the dining table. I also like this prayer from the Vedas : *Aum annapate annasya no dehyanamivasya shushminah, prapra dataram tarish oorjam no dhehi dvipade chatushpade*. It means, may the food I eat be beneficial for my body and may every one be blessed with food.

After giving a long description of the various types of austerities and services performed for self-realization and God-realization, Sri Kṛṣṇa tells Arjuna that all types of services should be dedicated to God with the holy words of dedication *Aum-Tat-Sat*. He tells Arjuna about the mysterious power of *Aum-Tat-Sat* which has been declared to be the triple designation of the Absolute Brahman. *Aum-Tat-Sat*—the three words—indicate one or the other aspect of the Supreme Divinity. The subtle power of *Aum-Tat-Sat* transforms each and every act into purity. These three holy words have specific spiritual powers. For that reason every type of worship should be performed with the consciousness of the Supreme *Brahman*. It gives sanctity to worship and also it is done with the spirit of respectful dedication. *Aum* is the holy syllable which represents the Supreme-Self. It is the original sound that envelopes the entire creation. The sound of *Aum* is the first expressive aspect of Supreme consciousness. It is the primordial sound of *Aum* moving within itself and interacting with *panch mahabhuta*—the earth, air, ether, water and fire which creates millions of forms and names in space and time. The holy syllable *Aum* represents the transcendent pure self which is the substratum of the entire universe. The universe has originated from the primordial word and primordial sound—*Brahma nada*. All the hymns in Vedas and in almost all other sacred scriptures start with the holy syllable *Aum*.

It is the primordial sound of *Aum* which was heard in deep meditation by ancient sages. The great mother *Gayatri* has been revealed from the holy syllable *Aum* and from Gayatri has been revealed the knowledge of the *Vedas*. *Vedas* are called *Sruti;* whatever was heard by sages in deep meditation is *Sruti*. All hymns of Vedas are the sounds revealed to the sages in yogic unity with *Para-Brahm*. The hymns of Vedas are *Srutis* and all other books written on the basis of Vedas are called *Smritis*. *Srutis* are the original words from the unified field of consciousness and *Smritis* are the remembered, processed information gained with personal experiences of the sages. Sound energy of the holy syllable *Aum* is a connecting link to the entire universe, as well as to the deepest mysteries of the Supreme-Self.

Sri Kṛṣṇa tells Arjuna that in the performance of any ritual and worship, the person should begin worship with the holy syllable *Aum* which initiates a sincere devotion, divine awareness with the absolute supremacy of the infinite and essential unity. It creates alignment with the source of life and invokes Supreme Divinity. The significance of starting worship with the holy syllable *Aum* is to experience the Lord Himself to be the essence of everything. In general, the knowers of *Vedas* know the techniques of perceiving a clear resonance of the sound of *Aum* in their mind. They begin every hymn in worship, with the holy syllable *Aum*.

Aum-Tat-Sat—is pure cosmic energy which connects us to everything in microcosm and macrocosm. *Aum* is the primordial sound that prevails at the heart of entire creation. The word *Tat* stands for the supreme reality in essence. *Tat* is the experiential knowledge and unity with the Supreme *Brhaman* in the performance of service; *Sat* stands for Truth behind everything and also for the work which is auspicious. Sri Kṛṣṇa declares that all types of worship, *yajña*, and austerity should start with the holy syllable *Aum* and completed with the dedicated words of *Aum-Tat-Sat* which indicates that worship has been initiated by the Lord Himself and is dedicated in His service. In this way the worship becomes purified and a means for liberation. Sri Kṛṣṇa has used the words *sadbhave* and *sadhubhave* which stands for nobility, honesty and purity of attitude in the performance of any worship and austerity.

Pure and honest attitude is always conducive to authentic spiritual growth, peace, happiness, clarified expanded awareness, fulfilment, harmoniously integrated lifestyle, self-realization and God-realization. While concluding the mysterious power of faith and *Aum-Tat-Sat,* Sri Kṛṣṇa repeats the genuine role of *sraddha* or faith in the progressive realization of the Supreme Divinity. *Sradha* signifies the honest faith which proceeds from yogic unity with the Supreme-Soul. As a matter of fact, a person's relationship with the Divine is primordial and perennial, but the individual perceives grace only in proportion to the degree of his faith, reverence and devotion. *Sradha* is the dynamic force that nourishes the mutual intimacy with the Divine. It illuminates the understanding of scriptural knowledge and makes it personal and experiential. *Sradha* strengthens love and devotion; purifies thoughts; unfolds inner capacities and sanctifies the entire attitude towards life. A meaningful, productive, creative and harmonious life begins with faith, willingness and acceptance. Faith in the Supreme-Self promotes faith in our own selves and in others. *Viswasa* or faith should be our *Swasa* means the breath of life. *Viswasa* is an honest effort of developing the most intimate relationship with God. It is the attitude or the *bhava* which matters the most in any type of austerity.

It is the sincere and selfless attitude in any pursuit that connects us with the ultimate reality. It is *sraddha*, the sincere faith and honest devotion, which gives peace, happiness, liberation and *nirvana*.

Most humbly we bow to Thee, O' Supreme Lord,
At Thy command moves the mighty wheel of time.
Thou art eternal and beyond eternity

— Atharvaveda 10.8.1

10

Surrender in God

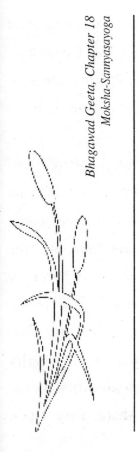

Bhagawad Geeta, Chapter 18
Moksha-Sannyasayoga

The dialogue opens with a specific question from Arjuna with reference to the concept of *sannyasa* (non-attachment) and that of *tyaga* (renunciation). Although Arjuna has heard about the words *tyaga* and *sannyasa*—many times during the dialogue but he could not understand the subtle meaning of these terms precisely. Sri Kṛṣṇa tells Arjuna that renunciation of all actions promoted by personal desires is *sannyasa*; while giving up the desire for fruit of actions is *tyaga*. The literal meaning of both words *sannyasa* and *tyaga* is to renounce; and both words are used in the sense of relinquishment, but *tyaga* is slightly different from *sannyasa*. It is the giving up of all anxieties related to the enjoyment of the fruits of actions. As discussed earlier, renunciation and the performance of action in yoga are essentially the same. Following the path of *sannyasa* without proper knowledge of *karmayoga* is not practical. A person cannot become a *sannyasi* by merely giving up the family life. *Sannyasa* is not simply a matter of changing into orange robes. It is a change in attitude both at physical and psychological levels of consciousness. It is the attitude of selfless action which prepares the person for *sannyasa*. A *karmayogi* steps into *sannyasa* in due course of time. There is no doubt about it.

Sri Kṛṣṇa tells Arjuna that *yajña*, charities and austerities should not be given up. These actions educate us in the path of self-realization and God-realization. These activities do accelerate our day-to-day emotions towards the goal of self-purification and help us to live in harmony with our own inner-self; with other people and with cosmic powers. *Yajña* and charity are blessings to the one, who gives and also to the one who receives. About charity *Vedas* declare *dakshinavante amritam bhajante* that means blessed are those who can give and share; they attain immortality in due course of time. A genuine renunciate does all his work in the spirit of detachment and gradually attains *sannyasa*.

Sri Kṛṣṇa declares that renunciation of obligatory actions is not proper. Obligatory actions include both, the daily duties at the individual level and also the special duties which we are expected to perform as a member of family and society. If we ignore these duties, our renunciation is immature. Anybody who neglects his obligatory duties disturbs the continuity of action in nature and brings about chaos in society. His renunciation is marked as escapism from the realities of life. He degrades himself and becomes a burden for himself and for others in the family and community.

He explains in detail to Arjuna, that when a person gives up the performance of actions due to the fear of physical and emotional discomfort; that renunciation is ignorance because he renounces his assigned duties due to the ordeal of effort it involves and also because of the fear of loss and failure. The feeling of escapism and pessimism originates from lack of self-reliance, self-respect and misunderstanding of one's personal duty. This type of renunciation brings more pain than any fulfilment or peace.

Genuine *sannyasa* is that which guides a person to the

acceptance of higher moral values with greater responsibilities. It gives him deeper satisfaction, and inner fulfilment. In true renunciation the individual performs all his duties as a husband or wife, as a doctor, teacher, soldier, without any feeling of 'I and Mine'. As a businessman he makes reasonable profits. He himself works very hard, and also likes to share his profits with his co-workers. His work reflects sincere devotion and the desire to serve others. It is the attitude of detachment which prepares him for the majesty of *sannyasa*. A renunciate lives a full life in the world, and performs all his assigned duties with a heart anchored to the Divine. This type of renunciation brings fulfilment, satisfaction, joy, acceptance and perfection.

Sri Kṛṣṇa glorifies and complements the person who has learnt to relinquish all desires for the rewards of his actions. He tells Arjuna that it is indeed very difficult for an embodied being to relinquish all actions completely; but the person who abandons the desire for the fruits of actions, is called a man of renunciation. So in order to become a relinquisher, the person has to learn to perform all his work with the attitude of detachment. He has to train himself into the gospel of selfless action.

It is indeed the attitude of selfless action that prepares the individual for total asceticism and renunciation. A true renunciate is emotionally integrated, determined and mature. He performs all his duties skilfully, faithfully, diligently and intelligently with an attitude of service. His actions become liberating and do not create any bondage in the present life or in the life hereafter. For him performance of his duty becomes a means for self-realization and God-realization. His life becomes enjoyable, purposeful and meaningful. There are always some genuine renunciates in every society, who perform their duties as a service to humanity and as a worship to Divine. They do not care for name or fame, or even salvation. Their work reflects the love of God, truthfulness, peace and harmony. It is the attitude of service that prepares the person for *sannyasa* and renunciation.

With reference to the philosophy of *karma*, and how we should perform our *karma* in order to live in peace and harmony, Sri Kṛṣṇa describes the nature of *Karma* and gives analysis of five factors which are usually present in the accomplishment of actions. Such as *adhisthanam* that means the body, the seat of action. *Karta* is the doer, *karana* means the instruments, in the form of sensory organs whereas *cheshta* is the conscious efforts and the fifth one is known as *daivam* which means destiny. Destiny is the software of all impressions, memories and (thoughts) *vasanas* that are recorded in the field of information known as the subtle body. It is the whisper emanating from the reservoir of memories that persuades a person into a specific type of activity. The mind recalls the information from recorded memories and initiates body into new actions. This whole process is very orderly and precise. Each and every memory comes to the surface of the conscious mind at a particular time in life in relation to the appropriate circumstances. The seed-memories are indeed the cause of new ideas and new actions. The lingering shadows of past actions of the previous lives and of the present are experienced as fruits and also in the form of some fleeting thoughts, which appear as flashes in the mind. Every embodied-soul has previous *samskaras* in the subconscious. The dormant impressions and memories are the chief factor in moulding the character and destiny of an individual. These latencies do remain dormant until favourable conditions instigate them into proper expressions on the surface of consciousness. The impressions and the latencies of the past are never lost. This storehouse of memories is indeed the destiny of man which expresses itself in the form of favourable and unfavourable circumstances.

Every single activity is an expression of thought which comes to the surface of conscious mind from the reservoir of *samskaras*. Everyone creates his own world from his own subconscious depths of memories, and builds his own personality which is wrapped around by his memories. The storehouse of memories is the destiny of man. Anyone who develops the ability to live in the awareness of the Self through meditation, can actually perceive the *samskaras* of the past, become fully aware of the present and can create a new destiny for himself. The yogis know very well, how the recorded data in mind operate in the field of action? That is why they recommend that we should learn to live in the consciousness of the Self and do our work with the guidance of the Supreme-Self. As long as we do not realize the presence of the supreme power we are bound to live like a poor victim in the hands of destiny, but when we become aware of the reality of our conditioned behaviour, we become the master of our thoughts, and the maker of destiny. A person has the ability to change the course of his *samskaras* by living in the consciousness of the Divine.

The play of destiny is within our control; all we need is to be aware of it. In this connection I like these words of Dr. Paul Brunton, "The difficulty lies in the persistence of strong mental habits which we have brought down from former incarnations, habits of false belief and of ignorant thinking which keep us tied to the 'not-self'. We are the creators of those habits; but since we have made them, we can unmake them. If their elimination were dependent entirely upon our own efforts, it might no doubt be a very difficult process to get rid of them, but we have help. The higher power exists. That will help you, but only after you have made strong endeavours of your own". A person has the ability to change the pattern of his *samskaras* by living in the consciousness of the Divine. The play of destiny is within the domain of every individual; the required effort is to be awakened to it.

After analyzing the five factors, which are generally involved in any work, Sri Kṛṣṇa tells Arjuna about the three-fold impulse which initiates all actions, such as *sattvic, rajasic* and *tamasic.* He explains the secret about the variety of results from different people for the same type of activity. For example, when the recipe of baking bread is given to a group of four, the results are always different, while they are given the same ingredients, the same instructions and the same necessary gadgets to bake the bread. This difference in results is due to the difference in their personal attitude and psychological make-up. It is indeed so true that the result of every action can be measured by personal attitude towards the accomplishment of the work. The personal touch, the feelings and sentiments are reflected in every kind of work. The attitude of a person plays a very significant role in the quality of the work which is produced. It reflects the quality of thoughts and the quality of thoughts are the clear reflection of the degree of self-awareness. For example, a *sattvic* person who is constantly connected with the purity of the Supreme-Self, he becomes highly intuitive, peaceful and very positive. His projects are very well planned and systematic. He is very honest, enthusiastic, intelligent, and genuinely dedicated to the completion of his work. His work plans are executed with grace and style, etiquette, orderliness and personal dedicated efforts yet devoid of attachments. He does everything very peacefully, devotedly while keeping in mind the welfare of others. The style of his performance is very relaxed, natural, effortless and spontaneous. He knows how to integrate different impulses and adjust his work according to the changing circumstances of life. He maintains a balanced state of mind, both in success and in failure, loss and gain, and also in pleasure and pain.

A man of clear vision knows exactly the expectations of the family and the society in which he lives. He performs all his duties skilfully, intelligently and diligently. He knows the time when he should move forward towards the accomplishment of his project and also when he should sit back and relax. He is quite clear about the appropriate age and time in life, when he should prepare himself for partial renunciation and for total renunciation. A *sattvic* person structures his life style in such a way that even while he lives in a family and community, he maintains his inner integrity and remains anchored to the Supreme-self. He is familiar with the nature of his work and makes the right decision at the right time. A man of *sattvic* understanding remains conscientious about his involvement in any kind of activity, which is prohibited by the law and interferes with the rights of others. He performs all his duties while keeping in mind global welfare. He knows how to respect the code of conduct and acts in harmony with the laws of *Dharma*. He becomes increasingly cosmic conscious, vividly aware, and perennially lives in wholeness of the Supreme Divinity.

On the other hand, a man of *rajasic* (passionate) attitude is generally very restless, selfish and greedy. He moves with his plans like a tornado, and remains passionately attached to quick results. He is very ambitious, restless and performs his duties with a lot of stress and strain. His eyes are always set on quick rewards and unreasonable profits. He really does not care whom he hurts and how much he hurts in the fulfilment of his personal desires. He is always obsessed with the thoughts of accumulating, possessing and hoarding wealth by all kinds of means, ethical or unethical.

A person endowed with *rajasic* (passionate) attitude goes to the extent of exploiting others and sometimes he ruins the life of even the near and dear ones. He takes delight in acting contrary to whatever has been ordained by the authorities or spiritual men of wisdom. He ridicules honesty and avoids listening to the ethical code of conduct. Words such as *Dharma*, truth, honesty and humility disappear from his lexicon. A person of *tamasic* attitude is generally negligent, lazy and procrastinating. His resolves are wavering and superficial. He is unpredictable and unreliable. Since he doesn't care for himself, he doesn't care for others.

Human nature is a subtle blend of knowledge, ignorance, truth and illusion which are expressed through the *swabhava* (inborn nature) of the person—*swabhava tu pravartate*. It is the inborn nature which finds full or partial expression in all kinds of activities. In ancient days when people started living in small groups and started to form communities, they gradually realized that they had naturally divided themselves into four major categories. This division took place naturally, for the benefit of society.

Sri Kṛṣṇa tells Arjuna that human beings have always divided themselves into four classes. This categorization has taken place merely for the well-being of the person and the society. The system of division has helped the community. The four categories have been named Brahmin, Kshatriyas, Vaisyas and Sudras. This classification into four types of work-order has been defined as caste system. The word 'CAST' means 'role' or part a person is expected to play in a specific life-time. That specific role played by the person, becomes his assigned duty, born of his instinctive nature.

A Brahmin is an embodiment of *sattvikta* (purity). He serves as a role model of purity, simplicity, austerity, self-control, honesty, wisdom, respect for religious practices and the knowledge of the scriptures. He is expected to guide other people into a pure life style by establishing an example of his own. Brahmin is the one who lives in the awareness of *Para-Brahmn* and reflects the purity of the Supreme through his thoughts, words and deeds. His life style is expected to be simple and an epitome of renunciation, self-dedication, self-sacrifice and service to the entire mankind.

The other class is Kshatriya. The word Kshatriya is a

Sanskrit word. The expression *kshatitrayate ity Kshatriya-* means the one who protects others from *ksati* (injury) is a Kshatriya. The duty of kshatriya is to enforce law and order for the well-being of society. Protection of the country, society and community is the first and foremost duty of the *Kshatriya*. Whenever there is decline of ethical values, the Kshatriya (the warrior) class is expected to fight for the welfare of the society and nation. A Kshatriya as ruler acts as an embodiment of *Dharma*, and his life is dedicated to the welfare of his countrymen. The next on the scale of fourfold division is the Vaisyas, endowed with more *rajasic* nature. They are instinctively interested in business and trade. The fourth is that of the Sudras naturally inclined to manual work and maintenance.

Each station of duty is significant and important for the development of society. In general as we notice, that people in society are not equal in their intellectual abilities, capabilities and capacities, but each and every person is a substantial contributor of his unique abilities in his own special way and should have the opportunity to share his special talents as an expression of his inborn potential. The self-imposed classification of people in society has always helped the community in proper distribution of work according to the individual choice of every person.

Any organized society needs saints, sages, scholars and spiritual teachers for wise counselling in every day life and when the community is faced with conflict of duties; philosophers, educationists, scientists and doctors for further research and scientific development; administrators, soldiers and leaders for protection and management; businessmen and industrialist for trade and coordinating development, stewards, labourers and mechanics for manual work and maintenance. This classification in society proceeds from personal *svabhava*. This term literally means the conditioned-self. The reason why people select different types of work is because of their personal conditioned nature. Every person is guided by his own *svabhava* and finds inner satisfaction in the special field of action as initiated by his inborn nature. This classification in society is psychological and universal. It is created by the people, of the people, for the people.

I like these words from the great educationist Gerald Heard. He says, "it seems that there have always been present in human community four types of consciousness. The Aryan-Sanskrit sociological thought, which first defined this fourfold structure of society, is as much ours as India's". Sri Krsna has also emphasized the fact that the strongest desire of every human being is to be able to show and express himself honestly and genuinely. It is the full expression of his inborn nature which gives him maximum satisfaction, peace and fulfilment in life. A man who acts in conformity with his *swadharma* attains satisfaction and peace in the present life and in life hereafter. Sri Kṛṣṇa declares that by being devoted to one's own duty, a person can attain perfection and liberation. The Supreme Lord of the universe should be worshipped through dedicated performance of one's own duty. By performing our personal duty in the spirit of service we are blessed with self-realization and God-realization. There is a story in the *Mahabharata* which explains this. This is the story of a merchant, who actually performed his work as a worship to the Lord and attained God-realization. The merchant Tuladhara lived in the city of Varanasi. He was a businessman, and also a great saint. He conducted his business with honesty. His work became worship for him and a means of God-realization. On the other hand, a Brahmin named Jajali who did all kinds of austerities in the forest; yet remained confused and deluded for a long time. One day while the old Brahmin was praying to God for inner peace and liberation, a voice was heard saying "Jajali you are not honest to yourself. You are arrogant and lack inner purity. You must approach Tuladhara, a merchant in Kasi (Varanasi) for your final lesson in self-realization". Jajali felt surprised, but still decided to visit the merchant. He went to the shop and sat close to him for a few hours and watched the method of his dealings. Tuladhar received the Brahmin very respectfully and said: "I have heard about your difficult austerities in the forest, you are really great, tell me more about yourself and what can I do for you". Jajali, the old Brahmin, was really amazed at the remarkable insight of the merchant, and requested him for guidance. Tuladhar explained his endeavours of living in yogic unity under all circumstances and the attitude of devotion to his work. Jajali heard the entire sermon very carefully. After listening about the greatest secret of Karamyoga, the arrogant Brahmin felt spiritually enlightened and blessed. This reminds me of some beautiful lines from Dhammapada : "Not by matted hair, nor by lineage, nor by birth is one a Brahmin. An enlightened Brahmin is the one who is honest, truthful, humble and firmly settled in the consciousness of the Supreme".

The performance of duty definitely becomes a means of inner growth and self-realization when performed as an offering to the Divine. For a yogi, the place of his work becomes temple of the Lord, and his work becomes dedicated service. He lives like a sage while performing all the duties of life. The attitude of dedicated service prepares him for the majesty of *sannyasa*. As a matter of fact total detachment does not come necessarily at some particular age or at any particular time of life; it is a process. It is the progressive realization of the Supreme-Self. A dedicated *Karmayogi* grows into *sannyasa* even without his being aware of it. He becomes a *sannyasi* in due course of time. Anybody who lives his life in harmony with the rhythm of inner tranquillity, peace and contentment, the radiance of his contemplated moods, and alignment with the Supreme *Brahman* becomes reflected in his day-to-day activities. His yogic unity with the source of life awakens the soul consciousness and initiation into honest service of God and humanity. When consciousness of the Supreme-Self becomes more evident to a person the attitude of selfless service comes naturally and spontaneously. The attitude of dispassion and renunciation becomes more pronounced and the feeling of 'I and Mine' is replaced by 'Thou and Thine'. He lives his life with an unflinching faith in God and enjoys the assurance of Divine intimacy. It is the perennial consciousness of the infinite in thoughts, words and deeds which makes the realization of truth to be natural and effortless. The blessed awakened intuition and introspection persuades him into the service of his fellow beings. Such an individual cultivates the valuable work-ethics, and through the practice of *Karamyoga*, he becomes eligible for the majesty of going in complete *sannayasa*.

Sri Kṛṣṇa tells Arjuna that every person is incomplete until he surrenders in God and learns to live in the consciousness of Divine. Our inner conflict shows itself leaping in various directions, with repeated search for satisfaction and inner completeness. We move here and there in confusion in search of something which is not quite clear to us. Lack of confidence explains our insecurity, restlessness and inner emptiness. The radical cure for all these problems is surrender in God.

When we take refuge in God with love and devotion, we learn to go beyond the masks of the conditioned-self, the boundaries of mind and body. We learn to live in the awareness of the self and begin to change the self-defeating ideas and become more goal-oriented. We become confident, self-reliant and integrated. Surrender in God is the easiest way to self-transcendence.

After explaining all the profound mysteries of yogic unity and how by adhering to *karmayoga* a person becomes eligible for attaining Supreme bliss, Sri Kṛṣṇa answers the appeal made by Arjuna in the beginning of the dialogue. He says *"manmana bhava madhakto madyaji mam namaskuru mamevaisyasi satyam te pratijane priyo si me"*. These compassionate words of Sri Kṛṣṇa have moved the hearts of millions arousing genuine love, devotion and respect for His Supreme Majesty. He assures his friend Arjuna with the most intimate words, revealing once again his personal identity as the Supreme Lord of the universe. "O'Arjuna, have faith in Me, be devoted to Me, perform all your duties for My sake, I will always take care of you, this is My promise, because you are very dear to Me. He further says *"Sarvadharman Parityajya mamekam saranam vraja aham tva sarvapapebhyo moksayisami ma sucah"*. O'Arjuna you should not be confused—forget all about your mixed notions of *Dharma*. Take refuge in Me. Be in eternal union with Me, I will take care of you—I will liberate you from all your fears. Sri Kṛṣṇa knows very well that Arjuna is confused because of his mixed notions of dharma. *Dharma* is the realization of the indwelling Lord in every little wisp of thought and in every little act of life. It is to live a life in constant unity with the Supreme-Soul. The concept of *Dharma* becomes mixed, confused and complex when a person is consciously disconnected from the Supreme-Soul and screens reality through some fixed individualized, localized, egocentric ideas. It is the personal attachment to that notion or idea which creates disturbance in the spontaneous flow of guidance from the indwelling Supreme-Self and creates confusion.

Sri Kṛṣṇa is persuading Arjuna for making a complete surrender without any trace of reservation. It means shedding of all pretences and stripping of all the masks of conditioned-self. The idea is that as long as the individual soul *(jivatma)* clings to its separate self-created, limited egoist individuality, the person becomes bound to move along with the instructions of his conditioned nature; but when he surrenders to the Lord, he becomes a co-worker and co-creator of his circumstances. An individual feels helpless and weak as long as he lives under the slavery of his conditioned behaviour, but once he takes refuge in the Lord, the Supreme power takes care of him. It is only through the grace of the Divine that he is introduced to the secret codes of his programmed life and the programmer. He becomes intuitively awakened and receptive to the call of the indwelling-self and his different concepts of *Dharma*, his self-assumed notions about obligations and duties, start blending into one essential *Dharma*—accept to live in the consciousness of the Divine and experience his own immortality. It is the realization of *Sat-Chit-Anand*.

With words *aham tva sarva-papebhyo* Sri Kṛṣṇa assures liberation from all sins. It means the removal of all conflicting emotions and confusions. The expression 'sin' can be explained as thought which brings guilt, shame and emotional disturbance, but when our mind and body are anchored with the majesty of the Supreme-Self, these lingering shadows of guilt and shame disappear spontaneously and we feel purified and liberated. In process of *saranagati* means a total surrender in Lord, we are blessed with *prapti* that means a total acceptance from the Divine. The expression *aham tva sarva-papebhyo* is an assurance from Sri Kṛṣṇa; it indicates that the Supreme Lord personally takes care of our problems and emotional conflicts, if we willingly take refuge in Him and cooperate unconditionally. Here Sri Kṛṣṇa's love for Arjuna has become more explicit.

The love of God and the grace of God is inherent in every person, it just needs to be revealed. Surrender in God is the experience of unity with the Supreme-Soul. When acceptance of the Lord is confirmed and established, the grace of Lord comes naturally. This relationship is unique, and inexplicable. When our intimacy with the Supreme-Soul becomes experiential, we become more and more devoted to the service of Lord and live with the assurance of inner unity. I belong to God and God belongs to me, is the essential message of all spiritual disciplines.

Sri Kṛṣṇa also makes it clear that the knowledge of the Supreme-Soul should be shared with that person only who is receptive—likes to listen and comes forward with willingness and devotion. He tells Arjuna that it is wise to avoid useless discussions with the one, who is cynical, devoid of respect, arrogant and does not want to learn. The person who comes forward with willingness and faith, and is prepared to listen and learn should be encouraged into the knowledge of God-realization. It is the duty of an enlightened person to initiate his fellow beings into godliness and help them personally. When a sincere devotee becomes open to the inner-flow of divine grace, he serves as a channel of the Lord. He becomes a medium and other people feel receptive to his words. His thoughts, words and actions become instrumental in initiating and enlightening the lives of others.

Sri Kṛṣṇa glorifies the knowledge of the Supreme-Soul and assures mankind that anyone who will study, and teach the message of this holy dialogue will always remain very dear to Him. He makes it clear that the teaching of Divine knowledge is the highest form of service to the Lord. The message of Sri Kṛṣṇa reveals the secrets of *Brahma Vidya* as well as *Yoga Sastra* that means the science and knowledge of the Absolute Reality and the art of yogic communion with the Supreme-Self. It is the exposition of spiritual philosophy based upon yogic unity with the indwelling-soul. This yoga scripture is a never-failing source of timeless wisdom needed for guidance in every day life. Here Arjuna is guided step by step through the conditioned games of mind into clear and precise understanding of the Absolute. The teachings of the holy dialogue provide a profound insight into the working of human nature and also the inspiration to stay relaxed, focused and peaceful. It reconciles the *Yoga* of knowledge, devotion and action into one—The *Yoga* of total surrender in God. Living a life in the consciousness of the Supreme-soul and to do all the duties of life in the consciousness of the Divine is to attain the ultimate perfection in Yoga. It is initiation to the majesty of the Supreme-Soul. It is progressive realization of the Self.

Sri Kṛṣṇa is very well aware of the process of inner awakening and that is why after introducing Arjuna to the call of the Divine with total surrender, His immediate next question is: "O'Arjuna, Have you heard attentively whatsoever we have discussed so far. Did you understand the meaning of My message?"

Arjuna's answer, *smritir labdha,* is very significant. *Smritir* literally means memory-and *labdha* means regained.

Smritir is to remember something, which has been forgotten for some reason. It is the realization of primordial relationship with the Supreme-soul. I like these beautiful lines by a Sufi poet : *Jab se jalva dikha diya tune muhj se mujhi ko mila dia tune.* God-realization and self-realization are essentially the same. There are similar beautiful words by another Sufi poet: *Dariya ki mouj se lehar uthi, aur ulat kar behar se kehne lagi, mai tujh se huei aur tujh mae phana, mai aur nahi tu aur nahi.* It means the self assumed identification of the wave dissolves at the dawn of realizing itself as an integral part of the river.

This is an experience of *atmabodha* which means the knowledge of the Self, the awakened intuition which reveals the ultimate truth in a series of blessed insights, each leading the individual to increased awareness than the preceding ones. It opens the doorway to the deepest mysteries of life and actualization of our inherent spiritual potential. It is being awakened to one's own completeness. It is the experience of going back to the wholeness *(Purna)* in which the individual-soul finds unity with the Supreme-Soul. It is the communication of the *'nara'* with his eternal companion *'Narayana'*. It is the transmutation of limited identification into the unbound cosmic identification.

Arjuna who was earlier lost into the limitations of

mind and body, now wakes up to the majesty as controller of the situation. His mind which was plunged earlier in *vishad* (depression)—now wakes up into a blessed state of receiving *prasad* (grace). The *vishad* is changed into *prasad* of the Divine. Arjuna feels totally oriented to a new concept of life, relaxed and peaceful. His entire outlook is changed for the better. The words, *sthito smi gatasandehah karisye vacanam tava*, explain inner integrity, confidence and the spirit of dedicated service. The expression *karisye vacanam tava* indicates the feelings of total acceptance with willingness and faith. Arjuna bows to the will of the Lord and feels like a chosen instrument in the hands of God. He promises to follow the guidance with purity of thoughts, words and deeds. Arjuna's experience of receiving grace indicates his feeling of inner peace and tranquillity, in contrast to the turmoil of his previous emotions. He feels peaceful, confident, spiritualized, integrated, firm, focused and motivated in carrying the command of Sri Krsna. This is indeed an evolutionary awakening when the individual self goes into unity with the cosmic self, and the person looks upon himself as the perennial fragment *(amsa)* of the Divine and also a medium, meant to accomplish the desired work in cosmic evolution. Arjuna speaks these words of surrender from the purity of his heart and from the integral wisdom of transcendental unity. There is an identical expression in the Ramayana, *Nath kripa mama gatha sandeha, Ram charan upajehu nava neha*—the grace of the Lord has eliminated my doubts and delusions, now I feel totally surrendered in the majesty of the Lord.

Sanjaya also glorifies the phenomenal talk between *Vasudeva* (Sri Kṛṣṇa) and the enlightened soul *Partha* (*Arjuna*). He says that whenever he recalls his blessed experience of listening to the conversation between Sri Kṛṣṇa and Arjuna and remembers the cosmic form of the Lord, he goes into ecstasy of inner joy over and over again.

Sanjaya says that wherever there is the contemplative wisdom and the yogic power of Sri Kṛṣṇa, the devoted yogic unity and the practical efficiency of Arjuna in performing work; there is morality, welfare, unfailing righteousness, success, victory, glory, and everything else. The implementation of yogic power and the contemplated wisdom under the guidance of Higher-Self is required for any kind of success and progress conducive to the well being of society. Yogic unity and social service should move together. It is the unification of personal spiritualized, enlightened, efficiency in performance of work for global welfare. Every type of success is based upon the faith and guidance of the indweller. When the individual-self goes into unity with the Supreme-self then the yogic power of the Lord descends upon the person. It initiates, enlightens and inspires him to work in a copartnership with God. The yogic power assures victory, spontaneous well-being, morality and the establishment of *Dharma*. When the work is performed in conformity with the grace of Divine, the results are bound to be rewarding and beneficial. There is no doubt about it.

Excellence in the performance of work—is in direct proportion to the unity with the Supreme-Self. The concluding word of the dialogue is *mama* while the opening word has been *Dharma*; the entire message is enclosed in these two words *mama Dharma*-means my *Dharma*. Life on earth becomes peaceful, prosperous and instrumental for liberation only if we understand the meaning of—my *Dharma*. *Dharma* of every person is to remain in unity with the indwelling Lord and perform all the work in perfect harmony with the voice of the Supreme-Self. Living in *Yoga*, and working through uninterrupted consciousness of the Supreme is indeed the Dharma of mankind. Let the grace of Supreme Lord be perceived and expressed in whatever we think, speak and perform. May the teachings of Bhagawad Geeta bless everyone with power of enlightened love, devotion and true knowledge—restoring peace, happiness and harmony on earth.

Sri Kṛṣṇa Arpanam Astu

Shubham Bhooyat

ekam shastram devakiputra geetam

eko devo devakiputra eva

eko mantrasya namani yani

karmaya eko tasya devasya seva

Hari Aum Tatsat, Hari Aum Tatsat, Hari Aum Tatsat

Aum Shanti-Shanti-Shanti

WORD INDEX

—O—